The Kingfisher Book of
Planet
Earth

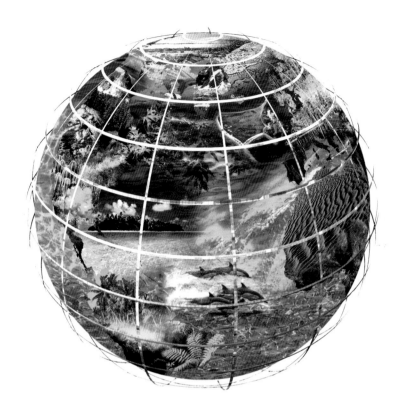

The Kingfisher Book of
Planet
Earth

Martin Redfern

KING*f*ISHER

KINGFISHER

Kingfisher Publications Plc
New Penderel House, 283-288 High Holborn,
London WC1V 7HZ

Author Martin Redfern
Series Editor Clive Wilson
Editor Rebecca Fry
Design Traffika Publishing Limited
Picture Manager Jane Lambert
Production Controller Richard Waterhouse
DTP Co-ordinator Nicky Studdart
Indexer Hilary Bird

First published by Kingfisher Publications Plc 1999

2 4 6 8 10 9 7 5 3 1
1 TR/0599/TWP/NEW/150NYM

A CIP catalogue record for this book is available from the British Library

ISBN 0-7534-0319-6

Colour separations by Newsele
Printed in Singapore

CONTENTS

Birth of the Earth

Five billion years ago, there was no planet Earth and no Sun. But the Universe was already in full swing and whole generations of stars had already used hydrogen to create the atomic building blocks – carbon, oxygen, silicon and others – that would later make up the planets. In a spiral arm of what is now our galaxy, clouds of these atoms started to condense, pulled together either by gravity or by shock waves from exploding stars. As they contracted, they began to rotate, forming a swirling disk at the heart of which lay a small, young star. And so the Sun began its life.

△ *Every culture has developed its own story of the Creation. This illustration from the Luther Bible (1530), shows God making the world and the Universe.*

Heat and dust

As the young Sun warmed, it blew a wind of energetic particles through the dusty disk, driving the remaining gases outwards to form the giant planets Jupiter and Saturn. Other dust grains accumulated into rocky lumps which bumped into each other, sometimes joining together. Slowly, the remaining material was swept up into a few large planets. One of these was the beginnings of the Earth.

Fire and brimstone

The new Earth was a hot young planet, warmed by atoms spewed out by an earlier generation of stars and by its own gravity. It suffered heavy bombardment from large asteroids and comets which rained down upon it, melting its surface. One of these impacts was so large that it created the Moon.

◁ *Hindu theory sees the Universe as an egg created by Brahma. Brahma emerged from the egg and split himself into two people.*

▽ *The collision of an asteroid with the Earth threw up so much rock that it eventually combined to form the Moon.*

Hard core

As iron-rich minerals were drawn towards its centre, the young Earth started to accumulate a great core of molten iron. This core now makes up 35 per cent of the mass of the Earth – the remainder is made up of less dense, silicate rocks. As it grew, the molten core churned around, generating electrical currents. These gave the planet its first magnetic field, which acted as a shield, protecting the Earth from radiation from space.

Living planet

Heat escaping from the core kept the surrounding mantle of silicate rock hot. Although this was solid, it flowed slowly, rather as ice does in a glacier, carrying heat to the surface in convection currents. Meanwhile, as the core continued to form, gases rose to the surface, contributing to the early atmosphere. What had been born was not a dead lump of rock, but a living, dynamic new planet.

▽ *The Earth is one of nine planets, along with numerous moons, asteroids and comets, that circle the Sun. The Sun itself is a minute dot on a spiral arm of the Milky Way, one of many similar galaxies in the Universe.*

Spaceship Earth

If an alien spaceship approached our Solar System and began scanning the planets for signs of life, it would soon detect that one planet was special. The atmosphere of the Earth is different from that of all the other planets. It contains plenty of oxygen but very little carbon dioxide. Closer examination would also reveal a protective layer of ozone, and traces of the pigment chlorophyll on land and in the sea — confirmation of the existence of life. The alien space probe might even pick up the incessant babble of radio and television transmissions, suggesting that the Earth's life is intelligent.

△ *Satellite sensors tuned to detect the pigment chlorophyll in plankton and plants were used to build up this image of life on land and in the sea.*

▽ *Infrared sensors reveal growth of new vegetation on the volcanic island of Fogo, near West Africa. The blue is surrounding sea, white the clouds and red the vegetation.*

Third rock from the Sun

The Earth is one of three planets that must have started their lives under similar conditions. Venus is about the same size as the Earth and a little nearer to the Sun. Mars is slightly smaller and further away. All three began with water vapour and carbon dioxide in their atmospheres. During their lifetime, the Sun has warmed. On Venus, this gave rise to a runaway greenhouse effect that boiled away any water. On Mars, the free-flowing water froze or escaped into space. Today, the surface temperature of Venus is over 400°C, while that of Mars is typically −100°C.

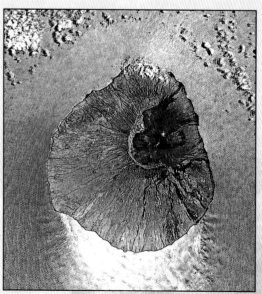

A living planet

Only on the Earth can life survive. The planet is a delicate ecosystem, maintained in a precarious balance between freezing and overheating. Yet, somehow, that balance has been maintained for billions of years, even while the Sun's heat has steadily increased. Many scientists now believe that the custodian of the planet is life itself. Thanks to life, the Earth's climate has not been disrupted by the warming Sun. Bacteria and algae, as well as plants, have consumed the carbon dioxide blanket that once enveloped the planet, and liberated the oxygen. In this way, they have sustained a perfect atmosphere for life to flourish — so far, at least. This concept is termed Gaia, after the ancient Greek Mother Earth goddess.

◁ An alien space probe would pick up all the signs of life on our planet — water, air and chlorophyll, as well as radio, TV and satellite signals.

The first view from space

The Apollo astronauts were the first to comment on the impact of seeing their home planet from space. In various ways, they all described it as breathtakingly beautiful, a fragile blue jewel in a star-studded sea of blackness. The first photographs of our planet from space also heralded a new understanding of the Earth from a global perspective.

Keeping an eye on the planet

The Earth is being observed from space at this minute — not by aliens (as far as we know), but by orbiting satellites. Remote sensing, as it is called, can reveal geological features too large to notice on land. The satellites can prospect for minerals in remote areas, monitor the atmosphere and watch weather systems forming. They can spot environmental damage and help us do our planetary housekeeping.

▷ Earth is one of nine very different planets. Mars (top left) is frozen under a thin, dry atmosphere. Venus (top right), by contrast, is hot under its thick, acidic atmosphere. Jupiter (bottom right) is a swirling bag of hydrogen with a small rocky core. And Saturn (bottom left), the other gas giant, has a ring of icy particles around it.

Sky and Sea

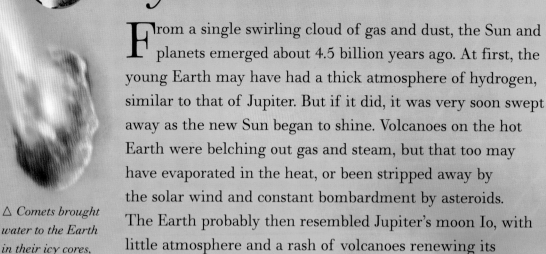

From a single swirling cloud of gas and dust, the Sun and planets emerged about 4.5 billion years ago. At first, the young Earth may have had a thick atmosphere of hydrogen, similar to that of Jupiter. But if it did, it was very soon swept away as the new Sun began to shine. Volcanoes on the hot Earth were belching out gas and steam, but that too may have evaporated in the heat, or been stripped away by the solar wind and constant bombardment by asteroids. The Earth probably then resembled Jupiter's moon Io, with little atmosphere and a rash of volcanoes renewing its surface. Slowly, the atmosphere and oceans that we know today emerged.

△ *Comets brought water to the Earth in their icy cores, and volcanoes released gases into the atmosphere.*

△ *Active volcanoes on Jupiter's closest moon Io are similar to those that formed the Earth's first crust more than four billion years ago.*

How the sea fell from the sky

The sky we know today probably came out of the ground and the sea must have fallen from the sky. Volcanoes were constantly adding nitrogen and carbon dioxide to the new atmosphere. And the Earth's oceans were created by icy comets returning from the outer Solar System and raining down on the Earth's surface. Even today, many thousands of tonnes of water fall to the Earth from space every year.

The changing air

When it was first formed, the Earth's atmosphere had no oxygen, only a lethal mixture of hydrogen, methane, ammonia and hydrogen cyanide. It must have been the worst case of pollution in history! But the hydrogen escaped into space and ultraviolet radiation from the Sun broke down the larger molecules, leaving a mixture of nitrogen and carbon dioxide. Only when life emerged and photosynthesis began did oxygen first appear on the Earth about 3.4 billion years ago. It probably was produced by organisms called cyanobacteria in colonies known as stromatolites, which can still be found today at low tide.

△ Colonies of billions of cyanobacteria, known as stromatolites, grow in Shark Bay, Western Australia. Ancient stromatolites may have released the first oxygen on the Earth.

△ Filaments of many tiny algal cells probably once filled the oceans, releasing oxygen into the young atmosphere.

A climate for life

By two billion years ago, the levels of oxygen were rising fast as algae filled the oceans. To produce the oxygen, the algae were consuming the carbon dioxide blanket that had kept the planet warm. But the planet did not freeze, as the Sun was also steadily warming. The two kept pace with each other, maintaining a suitable climate for life.

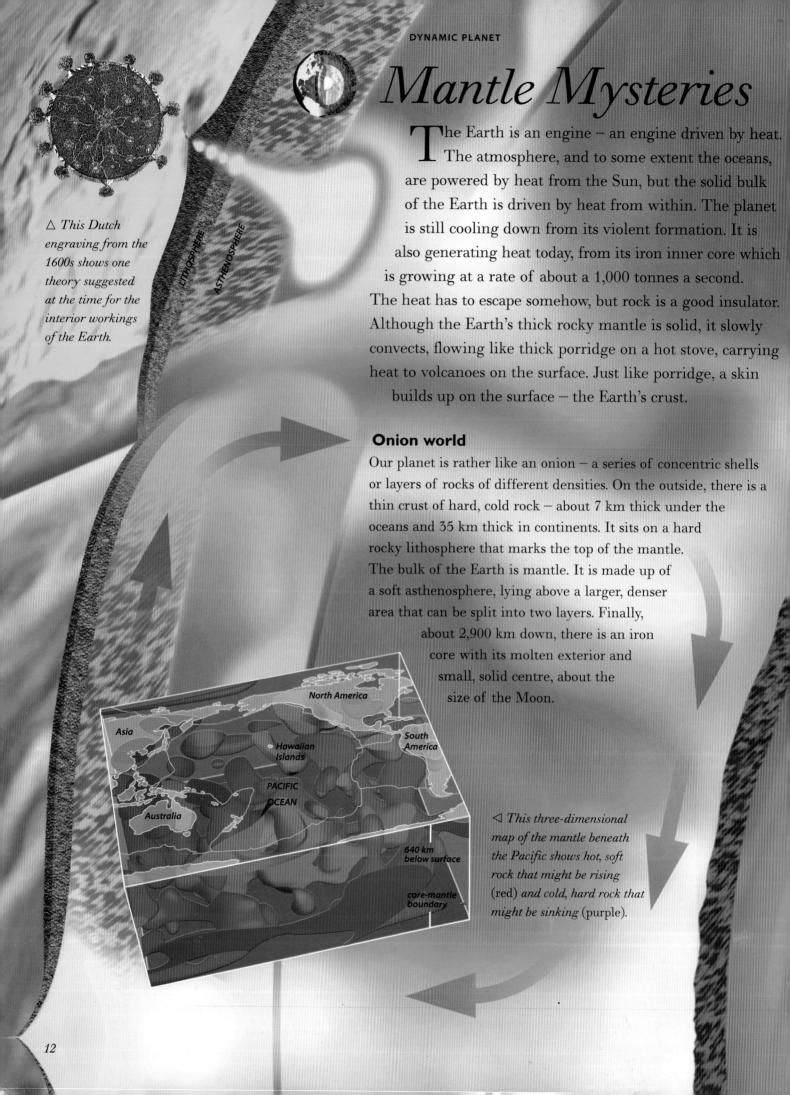

Mantle Mysteries

The Earth is an engine – an engine driven by heat. The atmosphere, and to some extent the oceans, are powered by heat from the Sun, but the solid bulk of the Earth is driven by heat from within. The planet is still cooling down from its violent formation. It is also generating heat today, from its iron inner core which is growing at a rate of about a 1,000 tonnes a second. The heat has to escape somehow, but rock is a good insulator. Although the Earth's thick rocky mantle is solid, it slowly convects, flowing like thick porridge on a hot stove, carrying heat to volcanoes on the surface. Just like porridge, a skin builds up on the surface – the Earth's crust.

Onion world

Our planet is rather like an onion – a series of concentric shells or layers of rocks of different densities. On the outside, there is a thin crust of hard, cold rock – about 7 km thick under the oceans and 35 km thick in continents. It sits on a hard rocky lithosphere that marks the top of the mantle. The bulk of the Earth is mantle. It is made up of a soft asthenosphere, lying above a larger, denser area that can be split into two layers. Finally, about 2,900 km down, there is an iron core with its molten exterior and small, solid centre, about the size of the Moon.

△ *This Dutch engraving from the 1600s shows one theory suggested at the time for the interior workings of the Earth.*

LITHOSPHERE

ASTHENOSPHERE

North America

Asia

Hawaiian Islands

South America

PACIFIC OCEAN

Australia

640 km below surface

core-mantle boundary

◁ *This three-dimensional map of the mantle beneath the Pacific shows hot, soft rock that might be rising (red) and cold, hard rock that might be sinking (purple).*

Endless cycle

The Earth is constantly changing.
New material is being added to the surface
only to be worn away and removed again.
Hot rock is rising up from the Earth's
mantle, while slabs of cold rock are
sinking back down into it. The entire
rock cycle is powered by heat
from within and sunshine
from above.

▷ *Lava erupting on the surface of the Earth may contain rock that has risen from the very base of the mantle – having begun its journey many hundreds of millions of years before.*

OUTER CORE

Lumps and bumps

As we travel over the surface
of the Earth, we see all sorts of
different features. There are continents
and oceans, mountains and valleys.
In some places the rocks are hard and
dense, in others they are soft and light.
Similarly, deeper down, within the
mantle and core there are also
differences from place to place
including lumps and bumps and
temperature variations.

Secrets of the Earth's interior

About 670 km down in the Earth's mantle, there is a boundary.
Old, cold slabs of ocean lithosphere descend towards it. Hot, soft
rock rises from it, towards volcanic hot spots on the surface.
Beneath it, the hot rocks also circulate. But does the whole mantle
circulate, or is heat passed between the upper and lower mantle,
without getting mixed up together? The answer could be that
both are true. Material sinking in the upper mantle comes to a
halt at the boundary, and spreads out for hundreds of millions of
years before avalanching on through the lower
mantle, almost to the top of the core.

◁ *Though made of solid rock, the mantle is slowly circulating. Boundaries at some depths cause the hot or cold rock to spread out before journeying on.*

INNER CORE

◁ *In the centre of the Earth is a solid iron core about the size of the Moon. Around it is a slowly churning molten iron outer core. Electric currents circulating in it generate the planet's magnetic field.*

Changing Continents

As mantle rocks slowly circulate, they bring lighter rocks to the Earth's surface like a scum. This has built up to form the continents, the planet's great landmasses. Like icebergs, there is much more to a continent than is visible. Continental crust can be 30 or 40 kilometres thick, compared to ocean crust which is only 6 or 7 kilometres thick. Although it is hard to find ocean crust older than 400 million years, the continents have been slowly accumulating ever since the Earth's surface solidified. Part of Australia, for example, is more than 3 billion years old.

△ This granite boulder, one of the so-called Devil's Marbles, is in northern Australia. Granite is made from sediments which have melted at great depths and risen to the surface.

Flotsam and jetsam

For billions of years, the continents have been tossed about on the mantle. Where they have crashed into each other, mountain ranges have formed. Where they have been pulled apart, oceans have opened up. When hot mantle rock rises under a continent, it can inject layers of volcanic rock, stretching the continent.

The rise of granite

As continental rocks pile up, the base of the continent gets buried deeper and deeper. As it descends, it heats up and the rocks at the base begin to melt and rise towards the surface. Huge bubbles of molten rock bake the surrounding rock which cools slowly, forming crystals. Eventually, the surrounding rock wears away to reveal a new material – granite.

▷ A technician from the US Geological Survey checks a 'creep' meter on the San Andreas Fault in California. It is sensitive enough to detect Earth movements the thickness of a human hair.

△ *New crust
forms along mid-ocean
ridges and moves aside, creating
the thin ocean crust that pushes continents apart
and dives down beneath them, forming volcanic mountain ranges.*

△▷ *About 200 million years
ago almost all the land formed
a single supercontinent. Since
then, the face of the Earth has
changed dramatically and will
continue to do so.*

▽ *Seismic waves, produced by the
26-tonne Vibroseis truck, bounce off
faults or hard layers in the rocks
and are picked up by detectors.*

△ *The Devil's Tower in Wyoming, US, is a volcanic plug.
First, molten lava solidified in the vent of a volcano. Then, the
softer flanks of the volcano eroded away, leaving the plug exposed.*

The continental waltz

If you look at the coastlines of the continents, you will
notice what seems like a remarkable coincidence — they
seem to fit roughly together. Africa, for example, slots
into South America. Align the edges of the continental
shelves rather than their present-day coastlines and the
fit is better still. This, geologists believe, is how the
continents were placed a 100 million years ago, before
the Atlantic opened up. Run the clock back further still
and you will find that 200 million years ago there was
a single supercontinent, known as Pangaea. It split
apart, opening up a new sea called the Tethys.

Under the Sea

More than 70 per cent of our planet's surface is covered by oceans. Their average depth is more than 4,000 metres – far too deep for sunlight to reach the ocean floor. Yet it is in the oceans that one of the most important clues to how the Earth works has been found. In the 1960s, as the ocean floors began to be surveyed by sonar, magnetometers and submersibles, it soon became clear that there is a whole system of ridges running down the middle of the world's oceans. This system is the longest continuous mountain chain on the planet – a network over 70,000 kilometres long, like the seam on a baseball. As the oceanographers discovered, the ridges are quite literally the seams of the planet, and the boundaries of creation.

△ Twenty Thousand Leagues Under the Sea *was written in 1870 by French science-fiction writer Jules Verne. It tells of a powered submarine,* Nautilus, *whose crew discovers weird and wonderful creatures at the bottom of the sea. One hundred years later, fiction became fact.*

Volcanoes beneath the waves

Mid-ocean ridges are peppered with active volcanic vents, from which dense, black basalt oozes like toothpaste into round lumps called pillow lava. The eruptions are not usually violent, but sometimes are accompanied by small earthquakes.

Black smokers

Water sometimes seeps into the volcanoes, where it dissolves minerals and then rises out of hydrothermal vents known as black smokers. The water can reach temperatures as high as 200° or 300°C, but it does not boil because of the enormous pressure.

Life around the vents

Amazingly, a whole ecosystem of organisms has been discovered around such vents. Bacteria that take energy from sulphur provide food for giant tube worms, clams, fish and blind white shrimps.

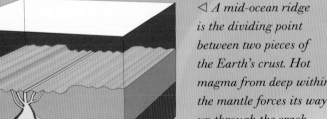

◁ *A mid-ocean ridge is the dividing point between two pieces of the Earth's crust. Hot magma from deep within the mantle forces its way up through the crack, continually creating new ocean crust.*

Recycling the ocean floor

If mid-ocean ridges are constantly spewing out new sea floor, does this mean that the Earth is expanding? The answer is no – the old ocean crust is sinking into the mantle. As the ocean crust cools, it becomes more dense and either dives into an ocean trench or under a continent, throwing up volcanic islands or mountain chains as it goes.

North
America

Europe

North
Atlantic
Ocean

Africa

South
America

South
Atlantic
Ocean

0   million years   180

△ *This magnetic map reveals the symmetry of the rocks on either side of the Mid-Atlantic Ridge, where rising magma has pushed the continents apart.*

◁ *The sulphur and dissolved minerals released at hydrothermal vents allow creatures to exist without sunlight.*

Earth Revealed

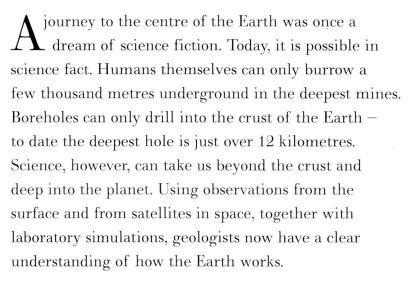

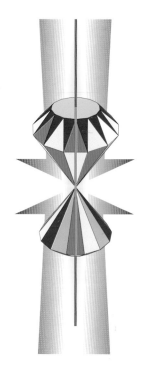

A journey to the centre of the Earth was once a dream of science fiction. Today, it is possible in science fact. Humans themselves can only burrow a few thousand metres underground in the deepest mines. Boreholes can only drill into the crust of the Earth — to date the deepest hole is just over 12 kilometres. Science, however, can take us beyond the crust and deep into the planet. Using observations from the surface and from satellites in space, together with laboratory simulations, geologists now have a clear understanding of how the Earth works.

△ *The characters in Jules Verne's* Journey to the Centre of the Earth (1864) *discovered living dinosaurs inside the Earth.*

▽ *The satellite* LAGEOS II *reveals variations in the Earth's gravity caused by different rock densities.*

△ *By squeezing a tiny sample of rock between the polished faces of two diamonds it is possible to re-create the pressures at the centre of the Earth.*

Squashed Earth

The Earth is very slightly squashed — its diameter at the equator is about 38 km greater than at the poles. This is because the planet is spinning, forcing material out towards the equator. Overall, however, the Earth is very smooth. If the planet were scaled down to the size of a one-metre ball, the difference between the highest mountains and the deepest valleys would only be a few millimetres.

Freefall

When Isaac Newton saw an apple fall, he realized that the force of gravity was pulling objects towards the centre of the Earth. What he did not know was that apples fall slightly faster in some parts of the world than others — although you cannot measure the difference using apples! Satellites, however, can measure the variations. The gravitational pull of a region of dense rock will make a satellite speed up. Over a region of lower gravity, it will slow down.

Split-second timing

The Earth is slowing down. We know from daily growth lines in fossil shells 180 million years ago that there were about 400 days in a year and each day lasted only 22 hours. This slowing down is caused mainly by energy lost as the Moon's gravity pulls on the Earth. There are also variations, of billionths of a second, that take place over days and hours, caused partly by currents in the core.

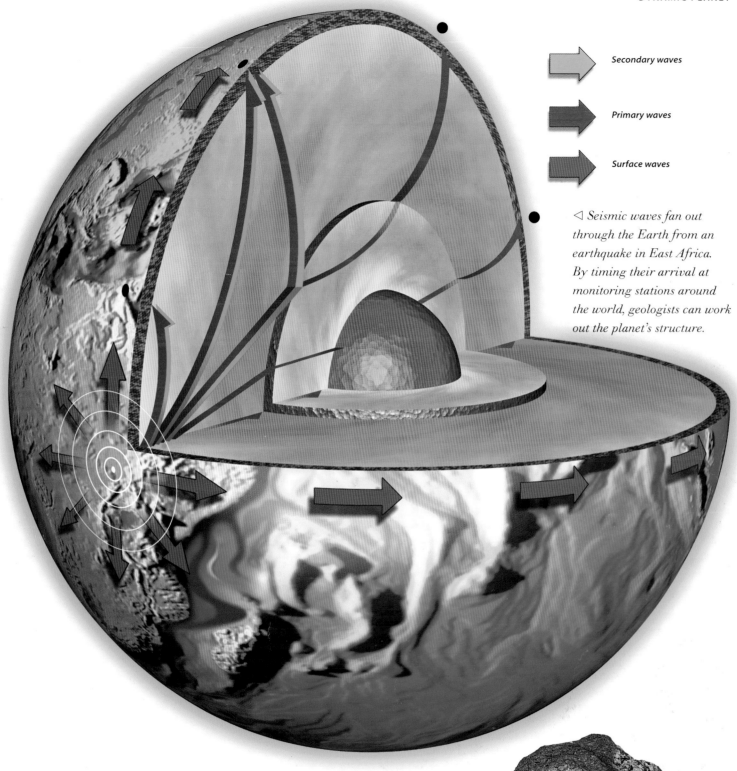

Secondary waves

Primary waves

Surface waves

◁ *Seismic waves fan out through the Earth from an earthquake in East Africa. By timing their arrival at monitoring stations around the world, geologists can work out the planet's structure.*

Planetary scan

Modern medicine can build up a three-dimensional picture of a person's bones and internal organs by scanning the body with X-rays or magnetism. A similar process can be applied to the Earth. Instead of X-rays or magnetism, geologists use seismic waves from earthquakes and nuclear bomb tests. The waves move quickly through hard, dense rock, but more slowly through soft rock. Computers then build up a detailed picture of the planet based on the routes the waves take through the Earth.

△ *This dense rock, made of the mineral olivine, is a sample of the mantle. It was brought to the surface in a volcanic eruption.*

The Living Core

By tracking the paths of seismic waves as they travel through the Earth after an earthquake, geologists have discovered some surprising facts about the planet's core. It seems to have a liquid outer layer that is churning like cement in a mixer at a speed of several millimetres a second. And right at the centre of the Earth there could be a crystal the size of the Moon! The pressure is so great at such depths that the only substance capable of behaving in this way is iron, perhaps with traces of nickel, sulphur, oxygen and silica. But geologists are puzzled by the discovery of a crusty boundary between the molten outer core and the mantle rocks above. What is this upside-down landscape 2,900 km beneath our feet?

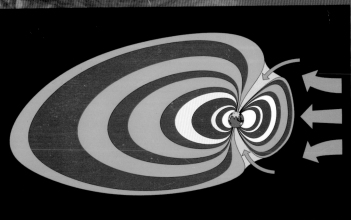

The Earth's magnetic field is rooted in the core but reaches far out into space. It envelops the Earth and protects us from harmful radiation and particles, especially those emitted by the Sun.

Lost oceans

This mysterious boundary is not continuous — in some places it is 200 km thick and in others absent completely. It could be an iron and silicate scum that has risen like continents to the top of the core. Or, perhaps, more likely, it is the final resting-place of old, cold ocean crust that has sunk down through the mantle — a lost ocean.

Upside-down mountains

The result is a subterranean landscape with mountains and valleys that dwarf any found on the surface of the Earth. Beneath Alaska is a liquid mountain taller than Mount Everest, and under the Philippines is a valley in the core that is twice the depth of the Grand Canyon.

△ *As charged particles from space stream in along magnetic lines over the poles, they strike the atoms and molecules in the Earth's upper atmosphere and cause spectacular light shows called auroras.*

Magnetic dynamo

The Earth's magnetic field originates in the outer core. It is far too hot down there for a permanent magnet. Instead, the field is generated by electric currents in the churning metal. Like any magnet, the Earth has two poles – North and South. At present, they lie in the Arctic and Antarctic, but evidence in the rocks shows that they have reversed positions many times in Earth's history.

Frozen in time

The inner core is about the size of the Moon, and growing! Iron is freezing onto it at the rate of about a 1,000 tonnes a second. Yet only about 4 per cent of the total core has frozen in 4.5 billion years. This change to a solid releases a lot of heat, which combines with radioactive decay to keep the outer core churning, the magnetic field working and the mantle moving.

▷ *If we could pull the mantle away from the core, a strange subterranean landscape of valleys and mountains would be visible on the underside of the mantle. The outer core – a liquid metal furnace, churning at temperatures of 5,000°C – pushes against these features, and affects the rotation and magnetism of the planet.*

Eruption!

Chains of volcanoes encircle the globe. Dotted along the edges of the plates that make up the Earth's crust, they are evidence that the interior of our planet is hot and active. When two continents move apart, material from the Earth's mantle rises to fill the gap. As the rock rises and the pressure drops, it partly melts to form liquid basalt. This lava emerges in huge quantities from fissures and vents – volcanoes – under the newly forming ocean. Occasionally, the ridges where the ocean crust is growing rise to the surface to form islands – Iceland is one example. Fresh volcanic land makes a rich and fertile home, but it can also be a risky place to live.

△ *The Giant's Causeway in Northern Ireland was formed from volcanic basalt which erupted as Europe split from North America 60 million years ago. The lava cooled to form these hexagonal columns, each up to half-a-metre across.*

An explosive history

The relatively sudden eruption of vast quantities of basalt must have taken place many times during the history of the Earth. There is evidence of other such events on the floor of the Pacific and sometimes on land, for example in Siberia and Argentina.

Sticky lava

When lava is rich in silica, it is sticky and does not flow easily. This causes pressure to build up in a volcano, until it erupts in a violent explosion of super-heated steam, ash and molten rock. This kind of volcano is the most dangerous, and its eruption hard to predict.

Types of volcano

It is tempting to try to classify volcanoes according to the way they erupt, but the geological record shows that any one volcano can change during its history. It may begin fairly gently, producing runny basalt at first. Over time, it will build up and gradually become unstable. Eventually, it will start to crack and fall in onto itself which causes explosive eruptions of viscous, silica-rich lava.

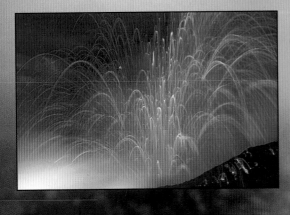

◁ *This spectacular firework display is in fact a volcanic explosion, caused as a flow of lava enters the sea off the Hawaiian coast. This lava has already flowed more than 10 km, yet its temperature is still 1000–1,200°C.*

Big bang

The biggest volcanic eruption in recent history occurred on the island of Krakatoa, Indonesia. The volcano had been silent since 1680 and the crater was plugged with solidified lava. Then, on August 27, 1883, the volcano exploded, blowing the entire island into the sky. Tidal waves up to 40 m high resulted – hundreds of villages were destroyed and up to 36,000 people died.

△ *This eight-legged robot was developed to explore other planets. But it has also been used on the Earth to collect samples of gas and rock from volcanoes too hazardous for humans to approach.*

Anatomy of a Volcano

Mount Etna is one of the most active volcanoes on the Earth. It has erupted at least 40 times in the last 20 years and shows no signs of stopping. Towering 3,300 metres above the Mediterranean in the east of Sicily, the volcano has four summit craters. During an eruption some of these craters can fill with red-hot lava. Seen from aircraft that pass overhead, these look like giant eyes in the night. Scientists have walked over every centimetre of the volcano with a variety of instruments. Seismographs measure the slightest shaking of the Earth while gravity meters and magnetometers measure the gravitational pull of rocks and their magnetic effects underground. Finally, scientists survey and measure how the mountain swells and contracts as the lava rises and falls within it.

△ *Carrying whatever they can, the population of a Sicilian village flees ahead of an advancing lava flow in this illustration from 1910.*

▽ *During the 1971 eruption of Mount Etna, a stream of lava slowly advanced down the slopes and engulfed the volcano observatory.*

Underground plumbing

From all these measurements, it is clear that molten rock collects in a wide, flat chamber about 20 km beneath the mountain and rises up a single pipe. Towards the top, perhaps 1,000 metres beneath the summit, the pipe splits, leading to four different summit craters and various other cracks and fissures. There is always molten rock at some depth in the central pipe, and this gives off bubbles of sulphurous gas, as if the volcano is breathing.

◁ *During the 1983 eruption of Mount Etna, lava surrounded the Sapienza Hotel. The flow moved slowly enough to allow people to be evacuated, and the building survived.*

Story of an eruption

The 1971 eruption of Mount Etna began like many others before and since. Magma in the central pipe reached the top of one of the summit craters, sending a fiery fountain of lava and hot rocks into the air. Lava then began to creep downhill at a slow walking pace. Then, about two months later, a minor earthquake opened up several vents lower down the mountain, draining magma away from the summit towards villages. Luckily, no one was hurt.

A change of mood

In the early 1990s, survey teams on the slopes of Mount Etna noticed a disturbing change. Not a rising bulge, as might be expected before an eruption, but a dip in the ground. Was this the prelude to a catastrophic collapse of one side of the mountain? If it was, then a landslide might follow, sending pressurized magma towards the city of Catania. Fortunately, the slope stabilized. But it showed how a volcano can change character dramatically.

△ *There are several types of volcano – a fissure, or crack in the ground (A); shield volcano (B); dome volcano (C); conical peak (D); composite volcano – like Mount Etna (E); and collapsed volcano or caldera (F).*

◁ *Beneath Mount Etna, rising magma pushes through a network of vents and fissures, leading to four summit craters and many cracks on its sides.*

△ *Mount Etna has been active since its birth, half a million years ago. On average, its lava flows are 12 m thick and can reach 7.5 km in length.*

Hot Spots

Around the Pacific Ocean is the Ring of Fire – a circle of volcanoes that marks the boundaries of the Pacific Plate. But not all volcanoes lie on plate boundaries. In the middle of the Pacific Ocean is the biggest volcano of all – Hawaii. The island sits on top of a hot spot – a spring of rising magma that has burst through the Earth's crust from the mantle below. The hot spot has been in the same place for millions of years. But during that time, the Pacific Plate has moved slowly to the northwest, passing over the top of the hot spot and creating a string of volcanic islands. The oldest of these was active more than 20 million years ago. The youngest is a submarine volcano called Loihi, lying beneath the waves, southeast of Hawaii.

△ This is a statue of the Hawaiian fire goddess, Pele, who is said to live in the crater of Kilauea.

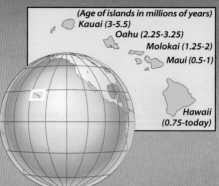

(Age of islands in millions of years)
Kauai (3-5.5)
Oahu (2.25-3.25)
Molokai (1.25-2)
Maui (0.5-1)
Hawaii (0.75-today)

△ The slow, northwesterly journey of the huge Pacific Plate can be seen in the increase in age of the islands as they move away from the hot spot.

◁ A night view reveals lava erupting along a fissure on the flanks of Kilauea and pouring into the sea.

△ Hawaii is entirely volcanic, with the peaks of Mauna Kea and Mauna Loa towering to 4,200 m. Kilauea is one of the world's most active volcanoes.

A Hawaiian eruption

Hawaiian volcanoes have their roots at a depth of 50 km or more. Lava rises up a pipe which broadens into a storage area a few thousand metres beneath the volcano. Tourists flock to Kilauea, the most active crater on the main island, to see an eruption. This usually begins with a curtain of fire as gas sprays up lava along a fissure. After a while, the runny basalt builds a cone around a single vent. Sometimes, lava streams towards the sea, crossing roads in its path.

Cooking a continent

There are many hot spots on the Earth. Some are beneath continents. One example is Yellowstone National Park in the US. Here, the continent is too thick for volcanic forces to break through, but heat still escapes, producing the famous sulphurous hot springs and geysers of the park. Another hot spot under East Africa is slowly cooking the continent. It has already created the Great Rift Valley of East Africa, and one day it may split the continent in half.

△ The chain of islands
stretching away to the northwest of
Hawaii represents eruptions of the past.
As the Pacific Plate moves northwest,
it carries the islands away from the
volcanic activity.

△ Many lava types can be found on Hawaii.
The distinctive ropey texture of pahoehoe
lava (top left) forms as scum on the surface
as a flow crinkles up. Aa-aa lava (bottom
left) has a rough surface. Very hot, fluid lava
(top right) can flow at a running pace.
And basalt erupting underwater
cools quickly to form pillow
lava (bottom right).

◁ A new volcano, called
Loihi, is rising beneath the
sea. From ocean floor to
surface is 3,000 m, but Loihi
still has another 900 m
to grow before it becomes
an island in its own right.

Opening an ocean

Geological evidence suggests that, before the Atlantic
Ocean opened, the crust of Europe was stretched by a hot
spot in the mantle underneath, and an ocean was nearly
created further east of where the Atlantic lies today.
It is this process that formed the North Sea and helped to
mature the oil deposits below it. When the Atlantic finally
did open, about 60 million years ago, it may have been
partly caused by the immense power of another hot spot.

Blowing its Top

△ *When Mt Pinatubo in the Philippines blew its top in June 1991, about two cubic kilometres of rock were turned to dust and sent high into the atmosphere, darkening the sky. Some dust spread around the world, creating spectacular sunsets and affecting the climate. But most rained down on nearby towns and villages leaving a thick layer of ash over everything.*

▽ *Super-hot pyroclastic flows of gas and lava raced down the flanks at 100 km/h, sending those people not already evacuated racing for safety. Here, journalists in a jeep flee from a giant cloud of noxious gases and dust.*

W hen old ocean crust dives down under a continent, it carries water with it. The rocks heat up, begin to melt and magma rises. But the water turns it into a giant pressure-cooker, waiting to blow its steam valve. On April 2, 1991, a nun walked into the Philippine Institute of Vulcanology and, begging their pardon, pointed out that the mountain behind her village had just blown up. Mt Pinatubo had lain dormant for 600 years and was covered with lush vegetation. The first earth tremors were followed by a plume of ash and gas, rising several kilometres into the sky. A rapid response force from the US Volcano Disaster Assistance Program rushed to the Philippines to monitor the eruption and warn the hundreds of thousands of people at risk.

Ring around the Earth

Two months later, a mighty explosion shot steam and ash more than 30 km into the sky above Mt Pinatubo. Nearly 300 people died, but had there been no early warnings or evacuation, the death toll would have been catastrophic. Following the eruption, a cloud of ash from the volcano spread out around the Earth, blotting out enough sunlight to lower global temperatures by half a degree over the next three years.

Eleven years earlier

One of the reasons why scientists could react so quickly to Mt Pinatubo lay on the other side of the Pacific, in Washington State, US. Eleven years earlier, in March 1980, Mount St Helens had also begun gushing steam and ash. Residents and loggers were evacuated and geologists flocked to the site. Instead of erupting out of the summit crater, a bulge began to appear in the northern flank. It grew to over 100 metres high and, at one stage, was rising by two metres a day.

Burning avalanche

At 8:30 in the morning of May 18, 1980, two sightseers watched as the entire bulge fell away during a mild earthquake. The lid was off the pressure-cooker! The volcano exploded sideways, sending a mixture of super-heated gas, steam and ash racing along a valley at more than 150 km/h. In all, a cubic kilometre of rock disappeared from the top of Mount St Helens. The two sightseers escaped with their lives and their camera, although 57 people died during the eruption.

▷ *Until May 18, 1980, Mount St Helens was a serene volcanic peak. But the pressure beneath was mounting.*

▷ *After the eruption, the mountain was 400 metres lower. About 540 million tonnes of ash and lava had erupted.*

▷ *As far as 30 km from the volcano, trees were stripped of branches, flattened like matchsticks or swept away.*

◁ *Molten magma inside Mount St Helens pushed a bulge out on one side of the volcano. When that collapsed, hot magma shot out sideways in what is known as a pyroclastic eruption.*

△ When heavy rain follows an eruption — as happened in the Philippines in 1995 — dust and ash turn to rivers of mud, adding to the disaster.

△ In AD79, hot ash from Mt Vesuvius buried thousands of citizens in the city of Pompeii. Casts of their bodies remain.

Volcanoes and People

Few people have ever seen the birth of a volcano. One exception is a Mexican farmer called Dionisio Pulido. On February 5, 1943, while preparing a cornfield for planting near his home in Paricutin, Pulido noticed that a strange pit in the corner of a field had a crack running across it from which gas was escaping. When glowing rocks were hurled out and nearby trees caught fire, he hurriedly departed. A day later, there was a cinder cone 50 metres high. After a year, this had risen to 325 metres, and eruptions of lava had covered two villages, leaving only a church tower rising above them. But this case is unusual. Most active volcanoes have been in existence for thousands of years, and lie in easily identifiable and comparatively small areas of the world. Yet people have always lived in their shadows and many still die in their eruptions every year.

△ Later eruptions of Mt Vesuvius have been less violent. This painting from the 1700s shows sightseers enjoying the pyrotechnic display.

▷ This map of recent volcanic eruptions shows how many volcanoes lie along plate margins where one plate is diving beneath another. Others occur where the crust is splitting, or over a hot spot in the Earth's mantle.

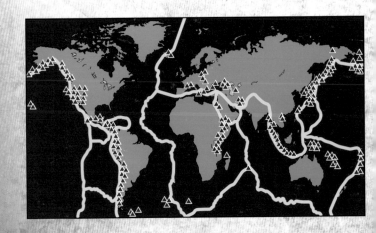

▷ *In 1902, when Mount Pelée, on the Caribbean island of Martinique, began to give out sulphurous fumes, people in the port of St Pierre did not evacuate because of local elections. A month later, the entire city and its population of 29,000 were destroyed (top right), apart from a condemned prisoner awaiting execution in his cell. On Montserrat (right), over 30 residents have died in eruptions since 1995 because they would not leave their homes.*

Pompeii revisited

The excavated remains of the crouched and huddled citizens of Pompeii are a grim reminder of the speed with which a volcano can overwhelm a population. In AD79, a 20-metre-thick blanket of burning ash and dust from Mt Vesuvius buried about 16,000 people living on its flanks. If the same were to happen today, three million people in and around the Italian city of Naples would be at risk.

Dangerous waters

Fire and water are a dangerous combination. Volcanic peaks are often covered in snow and the resulting mudflows, or lahars, can be more damaging than the eruption itself. At Nevado del Ruiz in Columbia in 1985, 22,000 people died as a 40-metre-high wave of mud burst down a canyon above the town of Armero.

Stopping volcanoes

There is no stopping a volcanic eruption, but the power can be redirected, away from humans. In Iceland in 1973, water was pumped into lava erupting from Helgafell, causing it to solidify before reaching the harbour and village. And in Sicily in 1983, explosives diverted a lava flow from Mt Etna away from tourist facilities.

△ *Volcano-watching can be an extremely hazardous profession. Here, a vulcanologist in protective clothing ventures to within metres of lava fountaining from a fissure in Iceland.*

Earthquake!

The surface of the Earth is paved with slabs of crust, floating on the dense, soft rocks of the mantle. But each slab is constantly on the move, as oceans open or disappear and continents drift like great ships on the mantle. Sometimes, one piece of crust dives down beneath another, or it grates alongside and gets stuck. Most spectacularly, two pieces may crash head-on. Where these mighty slabs meet, stresses gradually build up under the ground, and whole networks of cracks, known as faults, can appear. As the pieces suddenly slip into a new position, years of strain are released as an earthquake.

Tracking continents

The drifting continents can be tracked by flashing laser beams from them to orbiting satellites and measuring how long the beams take to reflect back to the ground. Typically, continents move at the same pace as your fingernails grow — a few centimetres every year.

△ *As the tension created by two plates rubbing together is released, shock waves ripple outwards from the hypocentre (A), causing an earthquake. The epicentre (B) is the point above where the waves hit the surface.*

▽ *A nearby earthquake measuring over 7 on the Richter scale will damage the foundations of buildings, rupture pipes, tear cracks in roads and even topple skyscrapers.*

▽ *The surface of the Earth may roll and heave for many days following a quake as aftershocks reverberate through the rocks.*

◁ A row of cars in a basement parking bay in Northridge, California, is squashed as the building collapses in 1994 during a quake, measuring 7 on the Richter scale.

◁ The San Andreas Fault stretches like a giant scar across the Carrizo Plain between Los Angeles and San Francisco.

The most famous crack in the world

Californians are used to living with the possibility of earthquakes. Their state is split north to south by a huge crack in the Earth's surface – the San Andreas Fault. To the west of the fault lies the Pacific Plate which is moving northwards, grating past the great North American Plate.

Earthquake intensity

Earthquakes can be measured on two scales. The Richter scale measures the energy of the ground waves produced by an earthquake. The Mercalli scale monitors physical effects on the surface. At the bottom end of both scales, the tremors are scarcely noticeable. At 5 on the Mercalli scale, doors swing open and liquids spill. By 8, masonry starts crumbling, roads crack and walking is difficult.

Changing places

The motion across the San Andreas Fault adds up to 34 mm per year, although it is far from smooth. Geological evidence shows that the fault moves during some quakes by up to 12 metres at a time. In 1906, San Francisco was devastated by such a quake. At the present rate of movement, Los Angeles will be as far north in 10 million years' time as San Francisco is today.

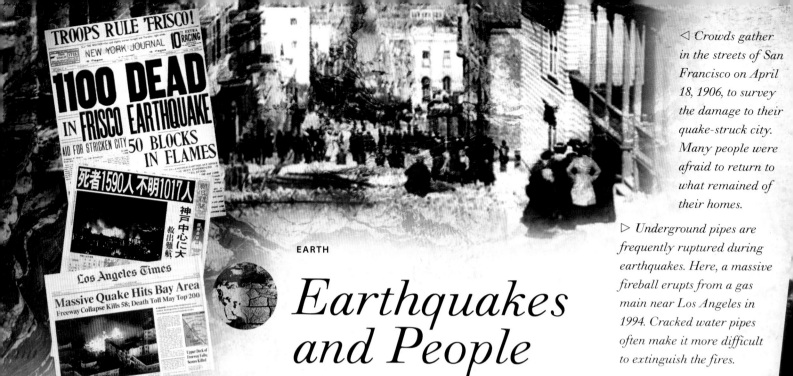

TROOPS RULE 'FRISCO!
NEW YORK JOURNAL
1100 DEAD
IN FRISCO EARTHQUAKE
AID FOR STRICKEN CITY 50 BLOCKS IN FLAMES

死者1590人 不明1017人
神戸中心に大
救出難航

Los Angeles Times
Massive Quake Hits Bay Area
Freeway Collapse Kills 58; Death Toll May Top 200

△ *Devastating earthquakes this century include the San Francisco quake in 1906, the Kobe quake in Japan in 1995, and the Loma Prieta quake in California in 1989.*

▽ *A giant crane lifts cars and debris from under the toppled Hanshin expressway in Kobe, Japan, after the quake in January 1995.*

◁ *Crowds gather in the streets of San Francisco on April 18, 1906, to survey the damage to their quake-struck city. Many people were afraid to return to what remained of their homes.*

▷ *Underground pipes are frequently ruptured during earthquakes. Here, a massive fireball erupts from a gas main near Los Angeles in 1994. Cracked water pipes often make it more difficult to extinguish the fires.*

EARTH

Earthquakes and People

Many small earthquakes happen every day. Big ones make headlines several times a year, and every so often an earthquake kills tens of thousands of people. No one knows precisely when a quake will happen, but we do have a good idea where. Some high-risk areas, such as California and Japan, are as well prepared as they can be. They have strict building codes, a well-educated public and emergency services which are constantly on alert. In Japan, some skyscrapers have heavy weights in the roof that can be quickly moved to cancel out the shaking during a quake. But in many earthquake-prone areas of Asia and South America, buildings are still poorly designed and there are few resources available to cope with a major earthquake.

▽ *This aerial view of Kobe reveals the devastation caused by the quake which measured 7.2 on the Richter scale. Black smoke rises above burning buildings. Fires can often cause more damage than the earthquakes that start them.*

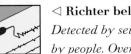

 ◁ **Richter below 3/Mercalli I**
Detected by seismographs, but not by people. Over 500,000 each year.

 ◁ **Richter 4.9-6/Mercalli VI-VII**
Felt by all. Furniture moves. People run outdoors. Some chimneys topple.

 ◁ **Richter 3-3.4/Mercalli II**
Detected by instrument and a few people. Delicate objects may shake.

 ◁ **Richter 6.1-7/Mercalli VIII-IX**
General panic. Some houses collapse, roads crack and pipes rupture.

 ◁ **Richter 3.5-4/Mercalli III-IV**
Obvious shaking felt indoors, walls creak, hanging items swing.

 ◁ **Richter 7.1-8.1/Mercalli X-XI**
Large cracks open up in the ground, landslides, few buildings remain.

◁ **Richter 4.1-4.8/Mercalli V**
Felt by most people. Some windows may crack and loose objects fall over.

 ◁ **Richter over 8.1/Mercalli XII**
Total destruction. The ground rises and falls in waves.

△ *The Richter and Mercalli scales plot the magnitude of earthquakes. The former measures wave energy, while the latter charts the effects.*

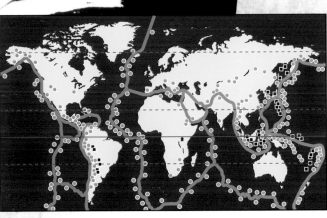

△ *Earthquake zones cluster along plate boundaries, which makes it possible to predict the location of earthquakes.*

Creating waves

By the time the San Andreas Fault reaches South America, it lies 200 km out at sea. This should be good news for the people living along the coast, but in May 1960, several big earthquakes along the fault line created one metre-high ripples in the ocean. As they travelled towards land, they grew to 10-metre-high *tsunamis*, or tidal waves. Three such waves hit the Chilean city of Valdiva, toppling buildings like sandcastles and tossing ships out of the harbour.

As safe as houses

Whether a building falls down in an earthquake depends on the strength and duration of the quake, and also on the building's design. In small buildings, flexible materials are better than rigid ones, and lightweight structures kill fewer people when they do fall. The most dangerous buildings are made of brick or stone, or have poor-quality reinforced concrete frames. They are often found in poorer countries.

Fire! Fire!

One of the greatest dangers during an earthquake is fire. Both in San Francisco in 1906 and Tokyo in 1923, more people died in fires than in the quakes themselves. Once fires start, they are often fuelled by cracked gas pipes. In San Francisco, 'smart pipes' are being developed that automatically shut off sections where a break is detected.

Urban dilemmas

When an earthquake strikes, the safest place to be is in flat, open countryside. The worst thing to do is panic. Nowadays, most people live in towns or cities, where falling glass and masonry outside can pose a real threat, so it is safer to stay indoors under strong structures such as stairways.

◁ *During the 1989 Loma Prieta quake, the flexible structure of the Golden Gate Bridge kept it standing, while more rigid bridges collapsed under the strain.*

Prediction and Prevention

△ *This is the very first earthquake detector, made in China, AD132. Earth tremors caused one of the balls to fall into a frog's mouth.*

Long before the age of scientific instruments, people watched for early warnings of earthquakes. The Chinese still look out for traditional warning signs such as strange animal behaviour or sudden changes of water levels in wells. Using such indicators, the city of Haicheng was evacuated in 1975, hours before a massive earthquake, saving hundreds of thousands of lives. A year later, 240,000 people died in Tangshan, where no warnings were given. There are many signs of an imminent quake, but the most reliable indicator may be the pattern of seismic waves that travel through the ground.

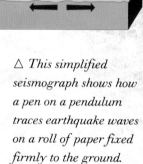

△ *This simplified seismograph shows how a pen on a pendulum traces earthquake waves on a roll of paper fixed firmly to the ground.*

High stakes!

Most big earthquakes are preceded by foreshocks. But nobody knows whether a minor earth tremor is an isolated event or the prelude to a major quake. From historical records, a big earthquake is predicted in the next 100 years – putting the chance of it occurring tomorrow at 1 in 36,500. However, the detection of minor tremors – suppose there are 10 of these a year – shortens the odds of a big quake in the next 24 hours to 1 in 1,000.

Real time warnings

Predicting earthquakes is difficult. But detecting them is easy. This fact was turned to an advantage in California, US, in 1989. Following the Loma Prieta earthquake, rescue workers were trying to free motorists trapped beneath a section of the Nimitz freeway. Debris was unstable and any aftershocks potentially devastating. At the focus of the quake, almost 100 km away, sensors transmitted a warning at the speed of light, so it reached the scene 25 seconds ahead of the shock waves, which travel at the speed of sound. This gave people time to scramble clear.

▽ *Tokyo school children, in fireproof headgear, emerge from their classrooms during a quake drill.*

△ *These Chinese government posters warn people of the strange animal behaviour to watch out for before an earthquake.*

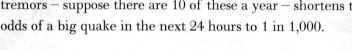

◁ *John Milne designed the first practical seismograph when he lived in Japan. On retiring with his Japanese wife to Britain in 1895, he set up the world's first seismic monitoring headquarters.*

P-waves

S-waves

Love waves

Rayleigh waves

Oiling the joints

No one can stop the relentless drift of the continents, and this results in earthquakes. But it may be possible to stop a big earthquake by causing lots of little ones. The longer an active fault line goes without a quake, the bigger the quake is likely to be when it happens. So if a fault line can be kept moving, a big quake may be avoided. The idea is to lubricate faults and this has been tested on a small scale at an old desert oil field in the US. By pumping water down abandoned oil wells, minor earth tremors were triggered, but not in the places expected. This makes it unlikely that this trick will be repeated in a densely populated area!

▷ *There are two types of body wave produced in an earthquake – Primary (P-waves) and Secondary (S-waves). These travel from the focus under the ground to the surface by either compressing and stretching, or shearing from side to side. Love waves and Rayleigh waves are L-waves, which cause surface effects.*

▷ *Laser beams shine out from this hilltop monitoring station near Parkfield in California. Timing the flashes as they bounce off a network of 18 reflectors on the other hills can reveal shifts of less than a millimetre over six kilometres.*

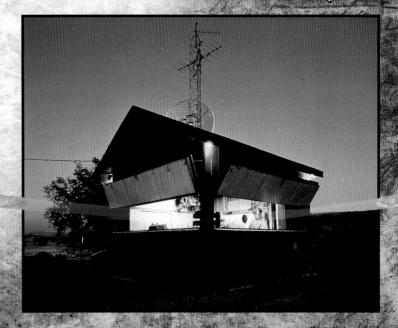

Mountains

The mighty continents are continually colliding with one another, but like a well-designed vehicle, they have crumple zones which buckle under pressure. Although made of hard rock, the layers in the continental plates fold on impact like a rucked blanket, rising from the Earth's surface to form mountains. These collisions take place over millions of years, as if being played out in extremely slow motion. As each layer piles onto the next, the mountains grow into great ranges.

△ These Jurassic limestone rocks at Stair Hole, on the south coast of England, are the result of Africa's collision with Europe 18 million years ago.

Mountains in the making

The continents are still slowly colliding, and the newest ranges continue to rise. Just 18 millon years ago, Africa drove Italy like a ramrod into Europe, creating the Alps. The Himalayas rose 5 million years ago during India's collision with Asia, and are still rising. This range contains Mount Everest (8,848 m), the world's highest mountain.

The birth of the Himalayas

Around 65 million years ago, huge volcanic eruptions caused the Indian sub-continent to split away from the other southern continents and to head northwards, pushing the great Tethys Ocean ahead of it. The dense ocean floor was pushed under Asia while the lighter seabed sediment was scooped up and squeezed between the continents, rising up like a multi-layered cake to become part of the Himalayan range.

△ Standing 4,808 metres high, Mount Blanc in the French Alps shows how much rock can be thrown up by an intercontinental collision.

Ancient collisions

The Himalayas and the Alps are the results of the most recent mountain-building activity. But there is also plenty of evidence of more ancient continental collisions. North America's Appalachian chain, eastern Greenland, the highlands of northern Scandinavia, and parts of Scotland were once joined in a huge range, the result of a collision that took place over 250 million years ago.

Completing the cycle

What goes up must come down, as the saying goes, and the Earth's crust records the history of a constant battle between the uplift of mountain-building and the forces of weathering and gravity. Little by little, the mountains crumble and, carried by rivers and glaciers, the sediment returns to the oceans. There it settles, only to be scooped up again several hundred million years later as a new mountain range is formed. And so the cycle continues.

△ *The Himalayas continue to grow upwards. But the taller a mountain, the steeper its sides and the more prone it is to landslides and the erosion of water and ice. After they stop growing, these mountains will eventually be reduced to the size of hills by erosion.*

△ *The Indian subcontinent heads north, 35 to 45 million years ago (1). Ocean sediments are scooped up and the ocean crust is forced under Tibet (2). The continents finally meet 5 million years ago, creating the Himalayas (3).*

The Wind

If left to itself, the air in the Earth's atmosphere would not change in pressure or temperature. But it is not left to itself. The Earth revolves, the Sun rises and sets, ocean currents warm or cool the air, clouds gather and scatter and mountains block the way. All this powers the atmosphere like a giant dynamo. As pockets of air become warm and expand, their pressure increases. This fuels winds which then blow to regions of lower pressure. At times, a wind can become so intense that it spins itself into a tornado or carves up the surface of the planet.

△ When two wind systems travelling at different speeds and in different directions clash, a tornado ensues. As the storm begins to spin, a funnel of warm air descends to the ground and a spiralling updraft sucks up debris.

△ This isolated farmhouse near Dalhart, Texas was photographed in 1938. By then, many farms had been abandoned as wind stripped away over-cultivated soil, turning the fields into a dust bowl.

Carved with sand

Air by itself may not seem like a powerful force, but when the wind whips up sand, it can cut like a chisel. Desert landscapes are almost entirely sculpted by wind. As well as carving rocks, the wind can pile sand up into dunes hundreds of metres high which advance slowly, engulfing villages and pasture.

Dust bowl

Away from desert sands, the soil is usually held fast by vegetation. But careless farming practices can change all that. In the Midwest of the US, it took centuries for prairie plants to evolve that could withstand the region's droughts and strong winds. Yet, within decades of the arrival of settlers, new crops and overgrazing had created a vast dust bowl.

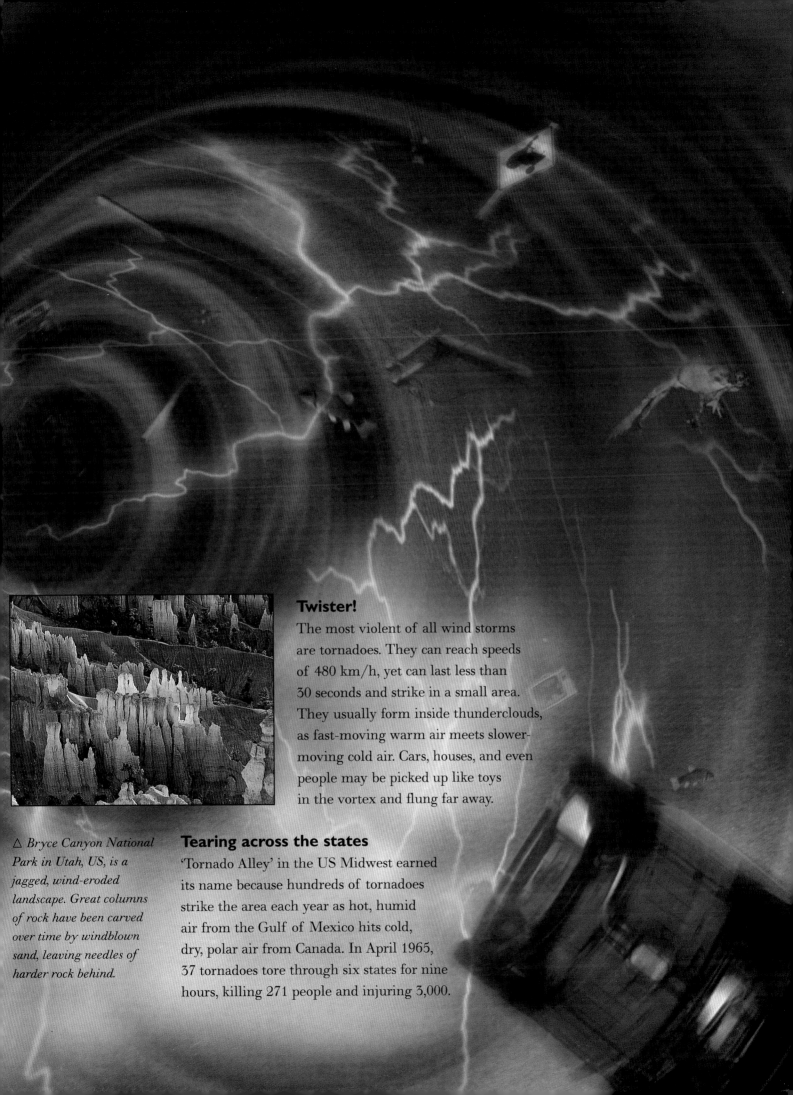

Twister!

The most violent of all wind storms
are tornadoes. They can reach speeds
of 480 km/h, yet can last less than
30 seconds and strike in a small area.
They usually form inside thunderclouds,
as fast-moving warm air meets slower-
moving cold air. Cars, houses, and even
people may be picked up like toys
in the vortex and flung far away.

△ *Bryce Canyon National*
Park in Utah, US, is a
jagged, wind-eroded
landscape. Great columns
of rock have been carved
over time by windblown
sand, leaving needles of
harder rock behind.

Tearing across the states

'Tornado Alley' in the US Midwest earned
its name because hundreds of tornadoes
strike the area each year as hot, humid
air from the Gulf of Mexico hits cold,
dry, polar air from Canada. In April 1965,
37 tornadoes tore through six states for nine
hours, killing 271 people and injuring 3,000.

The Weather

While the climate is all about the broad changes that occur from season to season and year to year in different regions of the world, the weather concerns local variations, from day to day and hour to hour. The world's weather systems are driven by the Sun which transforms our planet into a global solar-powered heat engine. Constantly warmed by the Sun, especially near the equator, air is pushed around the planet – it is this movement that creates weather. The world has three major circulation cells, systems where hot air rises continuously, cools and then descends. The first of these, the Hadley cell, is located over the equator. Hot air rises from this central band, moves to the north and south, then loses heat and drops. The second cell is found over the Tropics and the third over polar zones.

△ *A satellite wind-speed map of the Pacific shows slow winds in blue, medium-speed winds in pink and purple, and winds over 44 km/h in red and orange.*

△ *High in the atmosphere, where there is no friction with the surface of the Earth, jet streams blow around the rotating globe. This jet stream is shown by a line of high-altitude cirrus clouds.*

The front line

Weather is governed by regions of low or high pressure which form when masses of cold and warm air meet. When warm air rises, it leaves a low pressure hole, which is then filled by cold air. This is called a cold front. As the warm air rises, it also cools. The water vapour it holds condenses into clouds and the system starts to rotate. Each of these stages brings different weather.

Land and sea

The land and the sea have a major influence on the weather. When warm air passes over the ocean, it picks up moisture. If the warm air rises above the land during the day, it will draw in air from the sea, creating sea breezes. Then, as the air moves inland it passes over mountains or hills, where it cools. This causes clouds to form and eventually the moisture falls as rain or snow. In Asia, monsoons are caused by hot air rising over the Himalayas.

△ *Modern meteorology uses readings from an international network of land-based weather stations, atmospheric balloons and space satellites. Research aircraft such as this C130, nicknamed* Snoopy, *can fly into storm clouds and measure conditions at the heart of the storm.*

When the wind blows

Sometimes, in late summer when tropical sea temperatures are at their highest, hundreds of storm systems come together and rotate in a great low pressure system known as a hurricane. As the wind speed picks up, a hurricane will tend to move away from the equator, gathering force and whipping up high waves in the sea until it meets the coast, often with devastating results.

DIY forecasting

Anyone can forecast the weather. Simply look at what sort of day it is today and predict exactly the same for tomorrow. In mid-latitudes you will be right about 70 per cent of the time. But of course you will never predict the times when the weather changes. To do that, you need to observe the weather on one day in thousands of different places, understand the processes at work and calculate all the interactions that are likely to take place.

Predicting the unpredictable

Meteorologists enlist the help of supercomputers to forecast the weather. Using data from weather stations around the world they calculate what will happen up to ten days ahead. Even so, they are often wrong. This is because of tiny, unpredictable changes that eventually have dramatic effects somewhere else in the world.

△ *These light aircraft were overturned and tossed into trees by powerful winds of over 160 km/h during Hurricane Gilbert, which struck Kingston, Jamaica in September 1988.*

Weird Weather

The weather must be the most widely discussed natural phenomenon on the Earth. Usually, people are complaining about the cold, heat, drought or rain. In fact, our climate is remarkably constant and hospitable when compared to the extremes of heat and cold on Venus and Mars, or the 1,800 kilometre per hour winds on Saturn. Most of the surface of the Earth is a few degrees above the freezing point of water. Without that constancy, life on the planet would not continue so easily. Even so, the Earth's weather does create some strange, varied and often beautiful phenomena.

▷ *These may look like flying saucers, but in fact they are lenticular cloud formations photographed in Brazil in 1969.*

△ *This is one of many buildings in the French Pyrenees damaged when hailstones the size of tennis balls fell in June 1991.*

The clear light of day

Light waves of all colours shine from the Sun, but air molecules scatter mostly blue light, so the sky appears to be blue. When the Sun sets, its light travels through the dusty lower atmosphere which scatters more red light, making the sky look red. Light also travels at different speeds through air of different temperatures. Where cold air hangs above a layer of hot air, the light is bent and a heat haze is created. Occasionally, this will also magnify the image of a distant scene so that it appears as a mirage.

◁ *Layers of air of different temperatures spread light to produce this double image of an island. This sort of mirage is called a* fata morgana.

▽ On crossing mountains, layers of air rise, then fall to create a series of waves. As water condenses around each wave, layers of cloud are formed.

Flying colours

Falling raindrops can act like tiny lenses and will scatter white light into its spectrum of colours. So, if the Sun is shining on a showery day, we may see a rainbow. Anyone searching for gold at the rainbow's end will have a hard task since, were it not for the horizon getting in the way, a rainbow would form a circle and have no end. Sometimes a rainbow-like halo is visible around the Moon. This type of aura occurs when light is bent by ice crystals high in the atmosphere.

Raining cats and dogs

Occasionally, air currents keep hailstones in freezing clouds for so long that they grow to be several centimetres in diameter and cause considerable damage when they fall. There are also isolated cases of ice-blocks several metres wide hitting the Earth. Sometimes, very strange things have been known to have dropped from the sky, including beans, fish and frogs. The best explanation is that they were sucked up by tornadoes.

Thunder and lightning

During a thunderstorm, positive charges build up at the top of a storm cloud and negative charges collect at the base. Sometimes, the voltage is so high that the charge 'jumps' in a bolt of electric lightning, either to the next cloud, or to the ground. The heat of the lightning causes the air to expand so rapidly that it lets out a huge crack of thunder. The force of lightning can split trees, set fire to buildings and kill people.

▽ Circles of flattened crops can seem mysterious, but many are hoaxes. Others may be caused by mini whirlwinds.

The Climate

Although the weather in a region may vary from day to day, and from season to season, there is almost always a cycle that is repeated each year. The average weather an area experiences, season by season, year by year, gives us a measure of its climate. Meteorologists take into account temperature, rainfall, air pressure, sunshine, humidity and many other factors. Places around the Earth with similar climates can be grouped into nine distinct climate zones. These range from cold polar lands, to warm, wet equatorial regions, to hot, dry desert areas.

△ *Tree rings can reveal much about the story of our climate. In a warm year the rings that are laid down around the trunk are broad. Other years, when frosts are severe, there is less growth and the rings are thin.*

▽ *Rock carvings found deep in the Sahara Desert suggest that 7,000 years ago this area had enough rainfall to support humans and animals.*

The warming Sun

Climate is largely dependent upon the amount of the Sun's heat that reaches the Earth's surface. The Earth's rotational axis, running between the North and South Poles, is tilted towards the Sun – it is this that gives us the seasons. Depending on the angle of the Earth to the Sun, the areas closest to the poles receive different amounts of sunlight – so there are cold, dark winters and warm, light summers. The equator receives nearly the same amount of heat all year round and as a result its temperature varies very little.

Ocean currents

The Earth's climate zones are also affected by the oceans. The sea absorbs much of the Sun's heat, and ocean currents spread this to other areas. This is why the winter climate of Britain, in the warm Gulf Stream, is milder than that of Newfoundland, Canada, even though they are on the same latitude. Away from the heat-storing oceans, the interiors of continents always have more extreme temperatures.

Global greenhouse

Although a lot of the Sun's heat is absorbed by the land and sea, some of it is reflected back into space. But gases in the Earth's atmosphere act like the glass in a greenhouse and stop much of the heat from escaping. This greenhouse effect is responsible for fears about global warming, but it is also essential to life. Without it, most of the Earth would be about −15°C. Ice would cover the planet and there would be no life.

The world can be divided into nine main climate zones. They are polar (mauve), subpolar (light blue), temperate (light green), subtropical (orange), desert (yellow), tropical (dark green), equatorial (dark blue), subpolar (pink), mediterranean (red).

Sunspots

Sunspots, the dark patches on our star's surface, appear to have an effect on the Earth's climate. Between 1450 and 1800, sunspots were entirely absent. This coincided with a period that has been called the 'Little Ice Age' during which the River Thames in England froze over in winter and frost fairs were held on the ice.

◁ Climate shapes our planet and determines the landscape, vegetation and wildlife of each region.

Climate change

Alternating periods of hot and cold weather reach back through the history of our planet. Before the recent ice ages began 3.25 million years ago, for 250 million years it was consistently warmer than at present. Prior to this long period, there was a 100-million-year freeze. Changing carbon dioxide levels, volcanic activity or events beyond the Earth were all possible causes for these changes in climate.

△ All three forms of water – ice, liquid and vapour – are found on the Earth. Together, they help provide a climate that is just right for life.

47

Climate Threat

Since 1958, scientists have been monitoring the amount of carbon dioxide in the atmosphere from an observatory high on a mountain in Hawaii. They have found that the concentration of the gas has been rising every year. It is now thought that this is primarily due to the burning of fossil fuels such as coal and oil. But extensive forest clearance also releases carbon dioxide and makes the problem worse by removing trees that would otherwise soak it up. Overall, human activity is adding about 8 billion tonnes of carbon to the atmosphere each year, together with lesser amounts of other greenhouse gases such as methane, nitrogen oxides and CFCs.

△ *This image of Ferrybridge power station in England has been coloured to highlight the sulphur dioxide in the smoke.*

▽ *An aerial shot of the Brazilian rainforest reveals the extent of human damage. The forest shows up pink; areas cleared for agriculture are blue and green. The orange patch is a rainstorm washing away soil where the vegetation has been cleared.*

A global trend

Although temperatures vary from year to year, on average the Earth has been getting increasingly warmer over the past century. There is mounting evidence that this is due to the large quantities of greenhouse gases in the atmosphere. If greenhouse gas emissions continue at the current rate, temperatures will probably continue to rise, and the consequence could be a dramatic change in climate.

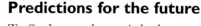

Predictions for the future

To find out what might happen to the climate in the future, meteorologists build models in supercomputers, rather like those used to forecast the weather. Most of their findings indicate that the world's overall temperature is likely to warm by two-and-a-half degrees over the next century.

Climate change

The effect of such a temperature rise may be profound. Deserts would probably become drier and coastal regions would grow stormier. The warm Atlantic Gulf Stream that brings heat from the Caribbean to western Europe would probably be disrupted too. Arctic water would not be cold enough to sink and return the flow south, like a conveyor belt. The circulation would stop and Europe would actually get colder.

△ *During an El Niño event* (top), *warm waters* (shown in purple) *reach the coast of South America* (right) *and prevent the cold nutrient-rich waters* (shown in blue) *from rising. Normally* (bottom), *an upwelling of cold water occurs and the winds push the warm waters east, towards Australia* (left).

Facing the consequences

The world's climate has, of course, changed in the past. The difference now is that human activity probably is responsible for the change, and humans – not dinosaurs – must face the consequences.

◁ *Greenhouse gases in the atmosphere insulate the Earth and prevent heat from escaping, raising the planet's surface temperature.*

El Niño

There is one ocean current that is already causing chaos with the world's weather. El Niño occurs when westerly winds reverse an ocean current in the South Pacific. This causes an accumulation of warm water off South America, and prevents the arrival of the cold, nutrient-rich waters that are needed to sustain wildlife in the region. As a result of El Niño there are droughts and storms around the globe.

△ *When slash-and-burn farmers move into an area they do just that, clearing forests, burning the timber and releasing carbon dioxide into the atmosphere.*

Water Power

The Earth is the only planet we know of where water exists in all three forms – ice, liquid and vapour. And in each of these states, water holds a tremendous power, both creative and destructive. Water is responsible for circulating the Sun's heat around the planet. Solar energy lifts vast quantities of water from the oceans to the mountains by vaporizing it, which causes it to rise. As it cools, the vapour condenses into the tiny droplets that make up clouds from where it falls to the ground as rain or snow. The rain becomes the rushing torrents of mountain streams and rivers. These are powerful forces which sculpt the landscape into hills, valleys and plains and carry rock particles back into the sea.

△ *Acidic rainwater has eroded limestone by dissolving it, leaving these towering rock formations in China.*

The great leveller

A downpour of rain can wash away huge quantities of sand and stone in one go. As the water races downhill, it chisels away at the rock, so eventually, over thousands of years, great V-shaped valleys are carved out. Once clear of the hills, the river slows and drops its sediment, creating a new path for itself. Some sediment is carried all the way to the sea, where it settles to form a wide, fan-shaped delta.

Dissolving rocks

It is not just the physical force of water that cuts into rock. As it falls through the air, rain dissolves carbon dioxide to become weakly acidic. This particularly effects limestone rock, which is dissolved by this type of rain. Over many years, whole networks of caverns and passages are carved out of hillsides. As the water flows, now saturated with dissolved calcium carbonate, it deposits this to form stalactites and stalagmites.

▽ *Clusters of stalactites slowly grow when water, saturated with dissolved limestone, drips from the cave roof. These may eventually reach to the floor.*

▷ *As it leaves the mountain, the speed and cutting power of the river decreases and it deposits soil across the plains, creating fertile lands in which to grow crops.*

Wave power

The awesome power of water flowing down towards the sea is matched only by the power of the water in the sea itself. Each metre of an exposed coastline receives about 50 kilowatts of continuous power in the form of waves. Picking up stones, then dragging them back again, waves constantly erode coastlines. Although wave power generators exist, none has been able to survive the destructive force of the sea. So far, no one has yet managed to harness wave power economically.

▷ *Water, warmed by the Sun, evaporates and rises into the atmosphere. The water vapour cools, forms clouds and falls as rain or snow. The force of gravity makes the water flow downwards and over many years it shapes the landscape.*

▷ *The Grand Canyon was cut into the dry rocks of Arizona, US, by the Colorado River. The system of canyons stretches for over 300 km and reaches a depth of 1,600 m in places. It slices through rock, some of which is 500 million years old.*

Floods and Droughts

Human life is dependent on water. We need it to drink and to irrigate our crops, and we harness its power to generate electricity. But if we lose control of our water supplies, if we find that we have either too much water, or not enough, the effects can be devastating. The world's oceans contain over one billion cubic kilometres of water. All the rivers, lakes and clouds contain just 0.03 per cent of that. Yet, a river in flood or a dried up river can mean the difference between life and death. Floodwaters can come from any direction – from above in exceptional rainfall, from a burst dam or in a freak storm from the sea.

△ *Huge guns were once used to fire dust into clouds, in a failed attempt to trigger rain over parched areas of Australia.*

Upsetting nature

In the natural scheme of things, a river will meander across its broad flood-plain, depositing fine sediment to make rich, fertile soil. But humans prefer rivers that stay in one place and build banks to constrain them. Mud becomes deposited on the riverbed and the riverbanks have to be built higher. Eventually, the river is raised up above the towns and farmland on its flood-plain. If heavy rain occurs, the river may burst its banks, flooding great expanses of land.

△ *Dams hold water to supply homes and fields, or to generate electricity. But a small crack in a dam wall can be catastrophic. The force of water behind it will turn a hairline crack into a giant hole in minutes. The result is a wall of water released into the valley below.*

◁ *A Sudanese farmer looks in despair at his parched land. The failure of the rains means that his family could starve.*

Storm surge

On February 1, 1953, storm winds and high tides combined to drive a wedge of water down the North Sea onto the coasts of eastern England, Holland and Belgium. Coastal communities were devastated, Dutch dykes were breached and the sea swept 60 kilometres inland. For Europe, this was exceptional, but in Bangladesh such flooding is a regular occurrence, causing homelessness and disease on a massive scale.

Drought damage

Excessive rain in one place is often balanced by drought in another. Many semi-arid countries rely on tiny amounts of rainfall to sustain crops. Their lands can only support a small population and are already overcrowded. When the rains fail entirely for a year or more, the result can be famine.

Future sea levels

If global warming melts the ice caps and destabilizes the western Antarctic ice shelf, the oceans could rise by more than ten metres. Even a one-metre rise in sea level would threaten low-lying coral islands such as the Maldives, as well as countries like Bangladesh and Holland. A bigger rise in sea level could easily leave New York, Bombay, London and Sydney under water.

△ *Just north of St Louis, US, (shown in pink and purple) the Missouri and Illinois Rivers flow into the great Mississippi.*

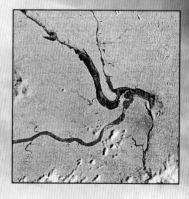

△ *In July 1993, the Mississippi River burst its banks (shown in blue and black), flooding an extensive part of the city.*

Lands of Ice

△ *Between 1645 and 1715, Europe experienced extreme winters in a period known as the 'Little Ice Age'. This engraving, from 1683, shows a frost fair held on the River Thames.*

One of the strangest features of the world that we inhabit is ice. No other substance has a solid form which is less dense than the liquid form. To put it another way, ice floats. So, when the temperature drops and the sea begins to freeze, the ice is on top of the ocean, not underneath it. That is good news for life, since the ice creates an insulating layer which prevents the rest of the sea from freezing. In past ice ages, notably one about 700 million years ago, when sea ice stretched to the equator, life would have died out had the oceans frozen solid. The effects of ice on land are different. As water expands to become ice, it can shatter a rocky landscape, and a large ice sheet can even push down a whole continent.

Waiting for an ice age?

Throughout the Earth's history, the temperature has fluctuated many times, perhaps due to changes in the Sun's activity or continental drift. The polar caps that exist today are a remnant of the last ice age, which began 3.25 million years ago. Since then, the northern ice sheet has advanced four times to cover large areas of North America and northern Europe. We may still be in an interglacial period today, waiting for the ice to advance once more.

Secrets in the ice

The polar ice caps carry clues to the past. By drilling out cores of ice, scientists can reconstruct the Earth's history. The thickness of the layers gives clues to the snowfall. Dust and chemicals in the ice keep a record of recent pollution and ancient volcanic eruptions. Trapped within the ice are tiny bubbles of the ancient atmosphere.

Rivers of ice

Although solid, ice can slowly deform and flow. Vast areas of the Antarctic ice sheet are in motion, carrying thick slabs of ice from regions of high snowfall downhill towards the sea. Once there, they eventually melt and are washed by the tides until giant icebergs break off, some of them as big as a small country. In mountainous regions, the snow packs harder and harder into ice, forming glaciers which flow down valleys, gouging out the rock as they go.

△ *Where a glacier meets the sea, there is a constant battle between ice and water. Sometimes avalanches of ice break off and crash into the sea, as has happened with this glacier in Alaska, US.*

△ When a glacier finally retreats from the landscape, it leaves deep U-shaped valleys, some so deep that they are flooded by the sea, creating fjords like this one in Norway.

▷ Like a frozen river, a glacier flows slowly through a rocky landscape shattered by ice. Lines of rocky debris build upon its surface as it gouges out a deep valley.

△ Air and water can sculpt icebergs into complex shapes. But 90 per cent of a berg is underwater, as ships such as the Titanic have found to their cost.

Changing Times

If the mighty continents are only the scum on the surface of our vast planet, sedimentary rocks seem even less substantial. They are literally the dust of ages, accumulated on the ocean floor then lifted up into mountain ranges. Yet, these rocks represent the history book of the planet, and within their pages, their layers, the story of life is told. The story is spelled out by fossils, but it is only in the last 100 years that we have started to understand them, and so have been able to read the story. Before then, our ancestors must have wondered what these strange shapes were. Perhaps they had grown inside the rock? Many Christians believed that they were the remains of creatures that had died in the Biblical flood.

△ *What events caused animals to either die out or alter dramatically? Was there a great flood after all?*

The fossil hunters

In the nineteenth century, William Smith, a surveyor, realized that similar layers of rock containing similar fossils occurred in different places, and that the sequence of layers was always the same. Sir Charles Lyell, now seen as the father of geology, argued that, because rocks formed at the same rate they do today, deep layers of sedimentary rock must be millions of years old.

Learning to read

As they looked closer, early geologists noticed that some of the fossil forms seemed to change subtly from layer to layer. If each layer was like a new page in the story of life, it appeared that the story was also divided into chapters. Between each chapter, there were clearly great changes in the creatures that inhabited the Earth. At last, they were able to recognize each chapter heading – the geological periods. The question remained as to what caused these changes.

▽ *By the time creatures such as this fish were swimming in the Earth's oceans, the planet was around four billion years old. Yet, the proliferation and diversification of life was only just beginning.*

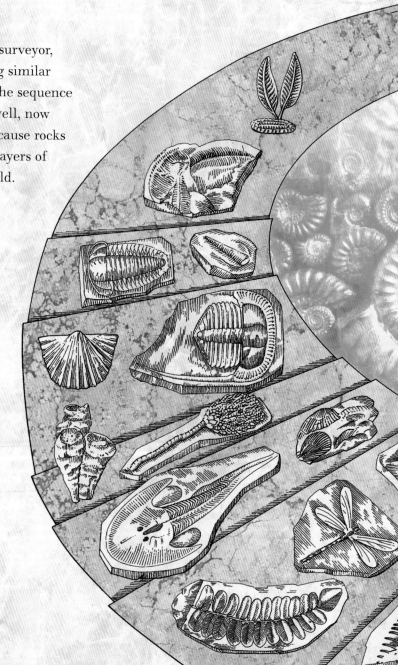

Numbering the pages

For many years, people have tried to estimate the age of the Earth. In 1650, an Irish bishop decided that the Creation occurred in 4004BC. By examining rocks, Victorian geologists thought that it was 20 million years old, a sensational suggestion at the time. Now, using radioactivity readings, we can put a much more accurate date on the rock layers of our 4.5 billion-year-old planet.

Ancient clues

For a long time, geologists believed that fossils were animals that had been turned to stone. We now know that even if this is not true, quite often the original molecules of life are still preserved in rock. Although it is not yet possible to recreate these creatures in a real-life Jurassic Park, they do give us invaluable clues to evolution.

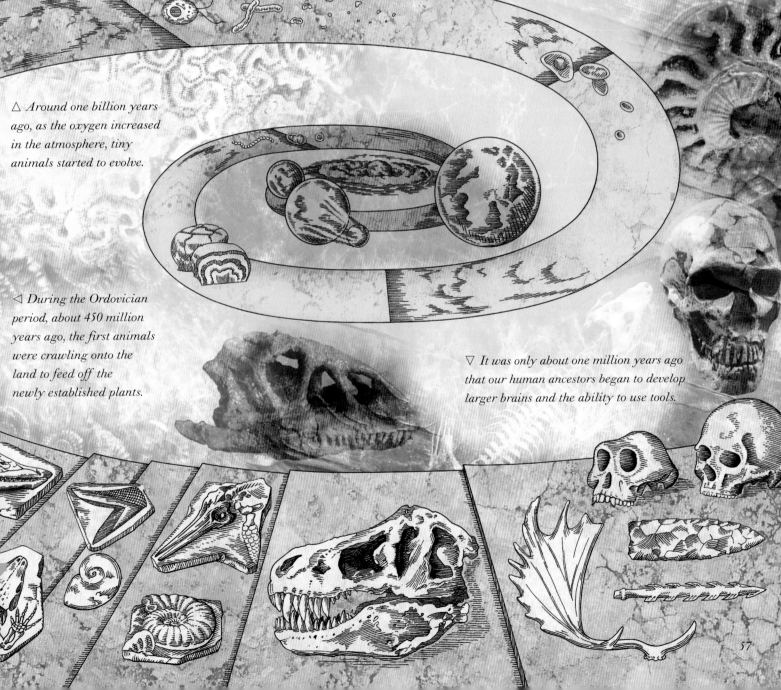

△ Around one billion years ago, as the oxygen increased in the atmosphere, tiny animals started to evolve.

◁ During the Ordovician period, about 450 million years ago, the first animals were crawling onto the land to feed off the newly established plants.

▽ It was only about one million years ago that our human ancestors began to develop larger brains and the ability to use tools.

The Dawn of Life

No one knows how life on the Earth began. Present-day life-forms seem far too complex and dependent on each other to have come into being spontaneously. But there are some new clues to suggest how and where life might have first arisen. Direct evidence in the fossil record is sparse, but research into chemical systems that can organize themselves, the discovery of new habitats where life can survive extreme conditions and studies of the genetic relationships of living organisms are all changing our understanding. In 1952, a chemist named Stanley Miller put methane, ammonia and hydrogen gases – thought to be components of the Earth's early atmosphere – into a flask containing some water. Through them, he sparked an electrical discharge to simulate lightning. By the next day, the flask contained amino acids, the building blocks of all life.

△ Charles Darwin's suggestion that humans had evolved from apes was greeted with a mixture of horror and ridicule.

▷ Darwin developed his theory of evolution as a result of observing finches on the Galapagos Islands. Their beaks had adapted to the type of food available on each island.

Building blocks

We now know that the early atmosphere was actually made up mostly of carbon dioxide and nitrogen, from which the chemicals of life form less easily. But they do form, and Stanley Miller's experiments began a whole new study into the chemical origins of life.

RNA world

There is a world of difference between a soup of organic chemicals and life itself. For life to get started, you need chemicals that can store information, reproduce and also have the ability to mutate. Today, most life-forms carry their information in genes made out of the chemical DNA. Although DNA would have had trouble reproducing on the young Earth, it may be possible for RNA, a simple version of DNA, to do so. Perhaps the start of life was an evolving chemical system based on RNA.

The early years

It is extremely difficult to read the history of life in rocks from the Precambrian, by far the longest period in the Earth's history. Nevertheless, microscopic traces of primitive bacteria and algae have been isolated. And, by the late Precambrian, there is evidence for much larger, multicellular organisms, which resemble jellyfish and worms.

▷ Some of the chemical building blocks of life may have been seeded on the Earth in meteorites. This one is mostly made of iron, but others are rich in carbon – an essential component of all life.

▽ This is one of the earliest fossils of a multicellular organism. Called Mawsonites, *it comes from the Ediacara hills of Australia and is about 700 million years old. It may have been a kind of jellyfish.*

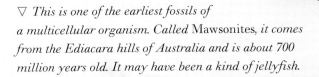

Fire and ice

Four billion years ago, when life was beginning, the Sun was weak and the planet may have been icebound. If so, life may have begun around volcanic springs deep in the ocean, or in pockets under the ice. In places, cometary impacts may have melted the ice. Warm pools may have been life's birthplace, on a scaffolding of mineral grains.

Alien invaders

At the time that life was getting started, our planet was still under bombardment from space. So, life may have been destroyed and reborn many times. It is possible that life did not originate on the Earth at all, but came from space, carried on comets and meteorites.

Wonderful Life

▷ *This small shellfish,
a brachiopod called
Lingula, is one of
life's success stories.
It has managed to
survive almost
unchanged for more
than 500 million years.
A present-day specimen
is almost identical to
those found fossilized
within Cambrian rocks.*

Well-preserved sedimentary rocks older than 600 million
years are seldom found, so fossils prior to this date are
exceptionally rare. Because of this, little is known about life on
the Earth before that period. After this time, however, the fossil
record reveals that something quite spectacular happened on
the planet. From the start of the Cambrian period, there is evidence
that the Earth was suddenly teeming with multicellular life-forms.
Most of the invertebrate groups in the world today also appear in
fossils, alongside a wide variety of creatures that seem completely
alien to us. This growth of new life was so rapid and diverse that it
has been called the Cambrian explosion.

A moment in time

Each of the many layers of shale and sandstone that
survive from the Cambrian period is evidence of the
past, recording what happened on the sea floor.
We might see the ripple marks produced by currents
of water, disrupted here and there by the tracks of
soft-bodied creatures that have long since disappeared.
By examining these tracks, we can determine the
behaviours and lifestyles of these ancient animals.

△ *Trilobites were around for
several hundred million years,
swimming in shallow seas
and burrowing in the mud.
The trilobite's closest modern
relative is the horseshoe crab.*

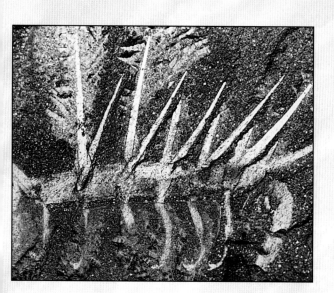

△ *This fossil creature from the Cambrian Burgess Shale seems so bizarre that it was named* Hallucigenia.

◁ *Many extraordinary creatures lived in the sea in the Cambrian period. Top left is* Opabina; *to its right,* Sanctocaris *and a jellyfish. Small arthropods feed off a dead trilobite on the left and along the bottom are sponges, corals and scaly creatures called* Wiwaxia. *Bottom right is the large crustacean* Canadaspis.

Meet the relatives

Much of our understanding of Cambrian life comes from the Burgess Shale in the Canadian Rockies. An amazing range of creatures has been found here and it is possible to recognize the relatives of crabs, insects, corals and worms that exist today. One creature, called *Pikaia*, looked like an animated anchovy fillet and could be our own ancestor.

Who's for dinner?

In one slab of rock, we can see the tracks of a trilobite, a predator that looked similar to an oversized woodlouse. The tracks lead up to the burrow of a small worm and you can still see where, one day 540 million years ago, the trilobite dug down into the burrow and had the unsuspecting worm for dinner.

Times of change

The fossil record shows that the course of evolution has been far from smooth and steady. Sometimes, there were great bursts of diversification, with hundreds of new species appearing over a short period. At other times, there were mass extinctions, probably caused by dramatic changes in the environment.

The Fossil Sky

For more than 500 million years, the Earth has been a generous host to life. But life has also changed the planet. Whether they are plants or animals, all living things are composed almost entirely of nutrients extracted from the earth and carbon from the atmosphere. Plants begin the process using sunshine to convert carbon dioxide and water into living matter. In consuming carbon, these organisms help keep the planet at a constant temperature. And when they die, they are re-absorbed into the earth to make new land and rock. Across the world, vast deposits of limestone and chalk are the end products of that process – they are, effectively, the ancient sky transformed into stone.

△ *Diatoms are tiny plant-like organisms that use carbon dioxide from the atmosphere for making food. The fossilized remains of these microscopic organisms form the rock diatomite.*

▷ *Carbon is the basis for all organic compounds including all living things and fossil fuels. Carbon is continuously recycled through the atmosphere, earth, plants and animals.*

Limestone

Many fossils are found in limestone, a sedimentary rock made from carbon, calcium and oxygen (calcium carbonate). There have been many periods in the world's history when thick deposits of limestone have formed. When there were no ice caps, higher sea levels and temperatures caused limestone to amass around the edges of continents and on flooded basins of land.

Carbon body-building

In these ancient shallow seas, the building materials of life were available in abundance. Vast quantities of calcium carbonate were used by microscopic organisms to build their intricate skeletons. The chalky White Cliffs of Dover, England, are made of the fossils of these creatures.

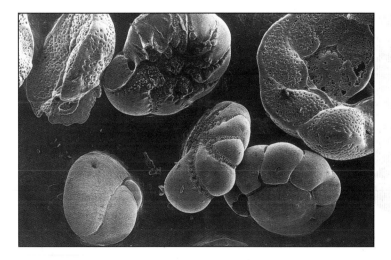

△ *Deep-sea muds are often entirely formed from the tiny skeletons of microscopic organisms such as forams. They are also found in limestones and preserved in deep-water shales.*

△ *The shells of these fossil brachiopods are made of calcium carbonate, which originally derived from carbon in the atmosphere. Fossilization happens when an organism is buried and its bodily structures are slowly hardened by minerals such as silica and calcite.*

◁ Radiolaria *are microscopic single-celled aquatic creatures, sometimes no more than one-thousandth-of-a-millimetre across. The shells of such minute creatures are among the most intricate of all fossils, and have complex structures of spikes, spindles and crevices.*

Climate control

If life did not consume carbon dioxide from the atmosphere, our climate might be more like that of Venus. There, a thick blanket of carbon dioxide traps the planet's heat and the surface temperature reaches 480°C. On the Earth, vast chalk cliffs and limestone mountains are reminders of just how much carbon has been turned into stone, ensuring that life has thrived.

Consumers of carbon

Larger organisms, such as corals and shellfish, make use of calcium carbonate to build themselves protective shields. Tiny plants, which feed on carbon dioxide, are eaten by copepods. These tiny animals then excreted the carbon into the sea.

Fossil formation

When an organism is buried in sediment, the soft parts start to decay, but the hard parts, like bones and shells, are often preserved. Compressed by layers of rock, other minerals penetrate the cracks and crevices and harden. The calcium carbonate structures that protected these creatures in life have helped them to survive as fossils.

▽ *In the past, people often identified fossils with mythical creatures. The curved shells of the oyster-like bivalve* Gryphaea, *found in many parts of Europe, were called 'devil's toenails'.*

Invasion of the Land

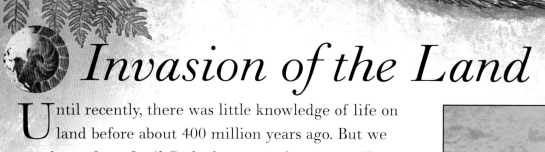

Until recently, there was little knowledge of life on land before about 400 million years ago. But we now know from fossil finds that more than 440 million years ago, plants, insects and other animals all grew, crawled or walked on the land. Plants were first to invade the land. In water, they had no fear of drying out, the water had dispersed their spores and brought them nutrients and provided them with physical support. The problem in water was that everything tried to eat you. Up above the waterline, a new, safe haven awaited colonization.

△ *Palaeontologists thought* Coelacanth *had become extinct 65 million years ago, until living specimens were caught off the coast of Madagascar.*

First land plants

During the Ordovician period, from 505-438 million years ago, plants took two steps towards a life on land. Firstly, plants such as *Sporogonites* grew simple roots. Then, a plant called *Cooksonia* developed stiff, hollow tubes, through which water and food could reach its upper parts. Later, plants reproduced using seeds, and giant ferns and gymnosperms populated Earth's forests.

▽ *An army of* Ichthyostega *pulls itself ashore in this scene from the Devonian period 365 million years ago. These early amphibians had seven-toed back feet and tails like fish.*

Giant woodlice and scorpions

Some of the first animals to follow the plants up onto land were insects. Millipedes fed on rotting vegetation, and predators such as centipedes sought them for lunch. With nothing much to hide from at first, some insects grew enormous. By 365 million years ago, one-metre-long scorpions and a two-metre-long relative of the woodlouse, *Arthropleura*, scuttled along the forest floors.

Fish with lungs

Since the Ordovician period, the seas have been teeming with fish. Bony plates were grown early on for protection, although predatory fish, such as *Dunkleosteus*, had powerful jaws to crush this bony armour-plating. For buoyancy, fish evolved internal gas-filled sacks called swim bladders. It is these that may later have become lungs.

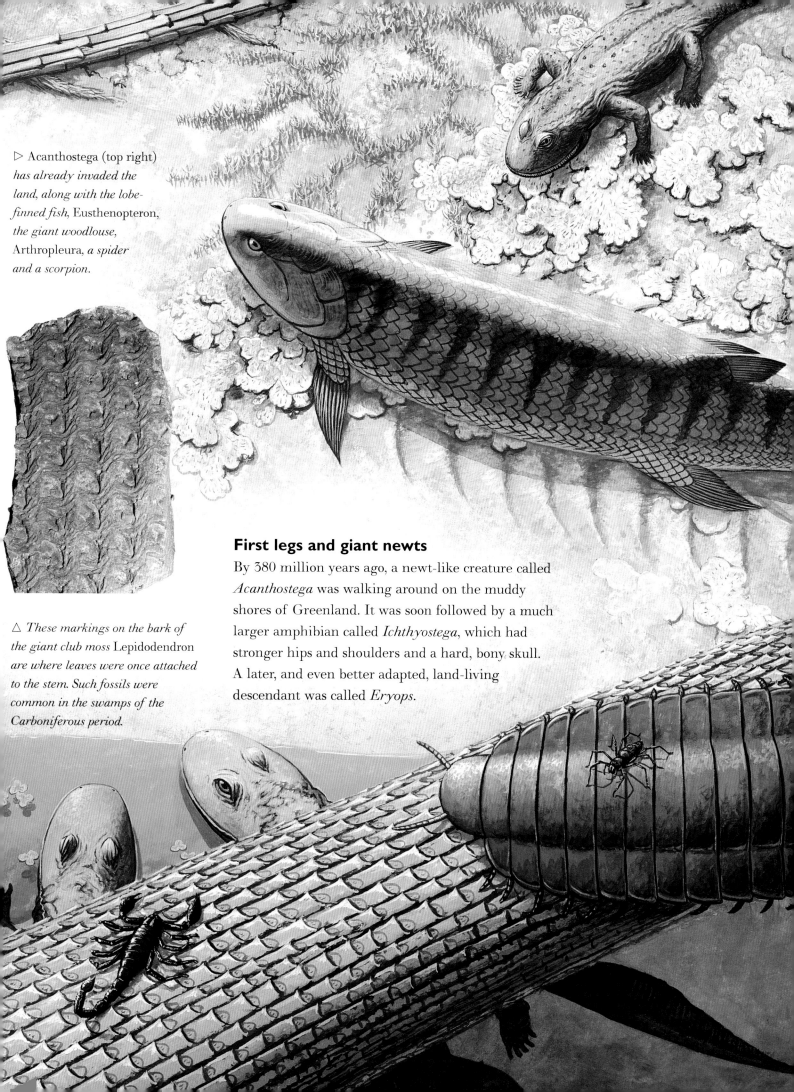

▷ Acanthostega (top right) *has already invaded the land, along with the lobe-finned fish,* Eusthenopteron, *the giant woodlouse,* Arthropleura, *a spider and a scorpion.*

△ *These markings on the bark of the giant club moss* Lepidodendron *are where leaves were once attached to the stem. Such fossils were common in the swamps of the Carboniferous period.*

First legs and giant newts

By 380 million years ago, a newt-like creature called *Acanthostega* was walking around on the muddy shores of Greenland. It was soon followed by a much larger amphibian called *Ichthyostega*, which had stronger hips and shoulders and a hard, bony skull. A later, and even better adapted, land-living descendant was called *Eryops*.

The Real Jurassic Park

By 205 million years ago, the great supercontinent of Pangaea had begun to break up. Between the continents of Laurasia to the north and Gondwanaland to the south, there was a new sea of warm, shallow water, the Tethys. There were no polar ice caps and the global climate was warm. This was the start of one of the most successful geological periods for life, and a period when dinosaurs became dominant. It was the real Jurassic Park.

△ *During the early 1800s, Mary Anning was frequently to be seen with her hammer along the Dorset cliffs near Lyme Regis, in England. She is said to have found her first ichthyosaur fossil at the age of 11.*

△ *These fossil bones make up one of the paddles or flippers of an ichthyosaur. The top (left) is made of fused limb bones, while the flexible part has evolved from the bones of the feet.*

Life in the sea

The Jurassic seas must have been thriving. A warm, tropical climate, plenty of nutrients, great blooms of plankton – all these provided rich pickings for larger life-forms. Jurassic limestones and shales lain down in those seas are full of fossil corals, sponges and shellfish – bivalves, gastropods and ammonites – as well as rarer fossils of reptiles and fish.

Sea monsters

Ichthyosaurs must have been the dominant predators in the sea. Although streamlined and similar to dolphins, they were not mammals, but reptiles. As were the long-necked plesiosaurs, with their powerful paddles and sharp teeth. Could it be that the legend of the Loch Ness monster is based on sightings of a living plesiosaur?

△ On land, a herd of browsing apatosaurs
is approached by a carnivorous allosaur.
A stegosaur (left) is safe behind its bony plates.

◁ This skull from a Jurassic ichthyosaur reveals
large eyes used for spotting fast-moving fish.

△ Ichthyosaurs
seem dolphin-
like, but the two
are not related.

◁ Plesiosaurs
were marine
reptiles, but
not dinosaurs.

More leg power

The earlier Triassic period saw a new kind of
reptile moving across the land – the dinosaur.
Unlike other reptiles and amphibians, which
have legs that come out of the side of their
bodies, the limbs of dinosaurs were underneath.
This enabled them to move faster and further, and
to grow bigger. In the Jurassic period, dinosaurs
inhabited almost all the land surface of the Earth.

Life on land

There were herds of massive sauropods such as *Apatosaurus*,
Diplodocus and *Brachiosaurus*. Some of them would each
have consumed a tonne of vegetation every day, and
inflicted considerable damage on the lush undergrowth of
ferns and horsetails and the forests of cycads and conifers.
But the sauropods were eaten by meat-eating dinosaurs
like *Allosaurus*, while overhead, pterosaurs wheeled and
small, agile dinosaurs ran about eating insects and lizards.

Kingdom of the Giants

During the Cretaceous period, dinosaurs ruled the Earth in greater numbers and with greater diversity than ever before. Growing big became a strategy for survival. While herds of huge *Apatosaurus* and *Triceratops* browsed in the vegetation, fearsome *Tyrannosaurus* and packs of agile *Velociraptor* preyed upon them. Overhead flew the biggest animals ever to take to the air, reptiles such as *Quetzalcoatlus*, with a wingspan the size of a small aircraft. Flowering plants were replacing ferns and cycads, and small mammals scurried through the undergrowth.

△ *Dinosaurs are classified into two main groups. In bird-hipped dinosaurs, two bones point back towards the tail. In the lizard-hipped dinosaurs, one points forwards.*

▽ *An* Edmontosaurus *has fallen victim to* Tyrannosaurus, *and a scavenger is already at work. An armoured* Euoplocephalus *(top left) has less to fear.*

Dinosaur log-jam

A broad river flood plain lay 145 million years ago in an area that is now part of the Rocky Mountains on the Utah-Colorado border. When the river flooded, some of the dinosaurs drowned and their bodies were washed onto a sand bar, creating a dinosaur log-jam. In 1908, more than 350 tonnes of fossil bones were taken from the site. Even so, the Dinosaur National Monument, as it is now called, still holds over 2,000 bones.

◁ *These flies have been preserved in amber for 30 million years. Genetic material has been obtained from insects twice this age, but it is poorly preserved.*

△ *In this scene from the film* Jurassic Park, *a baby dinosaur, supposedly reconstructed from fossilized genes, hatches from an egg.*

Warm-blooded?

One of the biggest arguments among dinosaur experts is whether dinosaurs were warm-blooded or not. Microscopic structures in some dinosaur bones are similar to those of warm-blooded birds and mammals today. This suggests that they could control their own body temperature. So perhaps some dinosaurs were not the cold-blooded monsters they are often portrayed to be.

Cretaceous Park

The film *Jurassic Park* implied that genetic material taken from blood-sucking insects preserved in amber could be used to reconstruct a living dinosaur. DNA has been recovered from Cretaceous insects found in amber, but it is likely to be damaged. Even with a limitless supply of perfect DNA from a living organism, mapping all its genes is a major task. For the time being, *Jurassic Park* remains fiction.

◁ *This claw bone from a dinsosaur called* Baryonyx *was found in Surrey in 1983. Its outer curve is 31 cm long. The claw would have enabled* Baryonyx *to hold onto wriggling prey such as fish.*

Extinction

The age of the dinosaurs came to an abrupt end 65 million years ago. Although individual species of dinosaur seldom survived more than a few million years, the group as a whole had persisted for 160 million years, showing a remarkable ability to specialize for many different ways of life. At the same time as the demise of the dinosaurs, 12 per cent of all families of marine organisms became extinct, as did many land plants. Clearly, something dramatic must have happened to affect so many forms of life so severely.

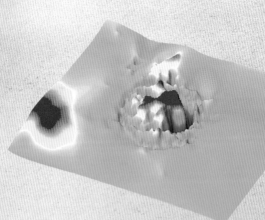

△ *This magnetic map of the Chicxulub crater off the coast of Mexico displays the 120-kilometre-wide structure left by a devastating meteorite impact 65 million years ago. Red, yellow and blue magnetic peaks reveal where strongly magnetized rocks rose up to replace sediment vaporized by the blast.*

A controversial theory

During the 1970s, Walter and Luis Alvarez were studying clay that dated back to the end of the Cretaceous period and found that it was rich in the rare metal iridium. The best-known source of iridium is outer space, leading them to suggest that a giant meteorite colliding with the Earth had caused the extinction of the dinosaurs.

▽ *Radar on the Space Shuttle reveals this 17-kilometre-wide crater beneath the sands of the Sahara Desert. It was formed several hundred million years ago and is one of many impact craters now identified.*

Cosmic impact

The Alvarez theory had little to support it – until, in 1991, a giant crater was found under the sea off Mexico. To cause such a crater, a meteorite several kilometres across, travelling at great speed, must have hit the planet. The impact would have released more energy than one thousand nuclear weapons, causing tidal waves and global fires, and been followed by semi-darkness for several years. It would have been a bad time to be a dinosaur.

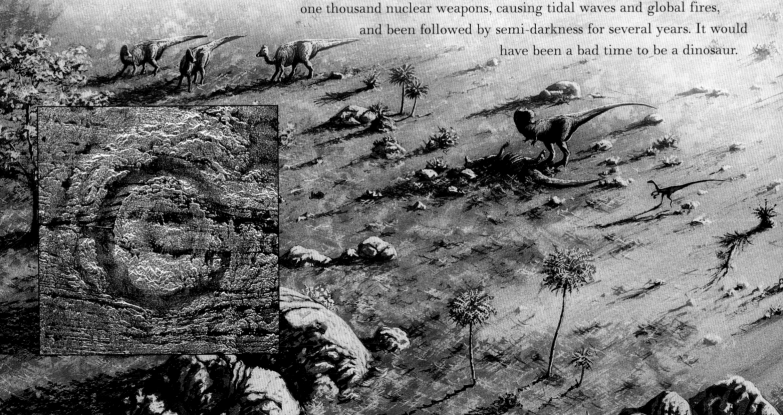

Threats and opportunities

Many rival theories have attempted to explain mass extinctions – but we can never know which one is correct. What we do know for certain is that the extinction of one group of animals is the evolutionary opportunity for another. It seems that the largest and most specialized organisms suffer most, as was the case with the dinosaurs. And 65 million years ago, the small, adaptable animals that were waiting for their big chance were the mammals. Today, another mass extinction appears to be in progress, but this time it is caused by human activity. Global warming and the destruction of habitats are set to send thousands of living species the way of the dinosaurs.

▽ *Grazing in what is now Mexico, herds of late Cretaceous dinosaurs look on in bewilderment at the flash of the giant meteorite. Their days are numbered – destruction and extinction will soon follow.*

◁ *Rock samples from the Caribbean act as a record of the meteorite's collision with the Earth. At the moment of impact, thousands of tonnes of seawater and rock rose into the air. This fallout eventually dropped to the Earth to form a distinctive white layer in the rock.*

The Birds and the Bees

In the late Jurassic period, 150 million years ago, in part of southern Germany that now lies just north of Munich, there was a warm, salty lagoon. Fish swept in by storms perished in its stagnant waters and sank to the bottom. A horseshoe crab staggered around, leaving spiral tracks, before dying. Anything that entered the lagoon perished, and the remains were preserved in the fine layers of muddy limestone. The fossils that have been found there are not only of creatures that crawled or were washed into the lagoon. Some must have been blown in by the winds, or even flown there.

First flight

In 1860, a single feather was found preserved in the rocks of what had once been the lagoon. It was the same shape as the flight feather of a modern bird. A year later, the complete skeleton of a feathered creature was found. It was named *Archaeopteryx*, meaning ancient wing. It had teeth rather than a beak, but it was winged, with a feathered tail, and clearly could have flown.

▷ *Creatures of all sorts have taken to the air, including mammals, reptiles (pterosaurs) and birds, the only group to develop feathers. Here, a flock of* Archaeopteryx *looks down on a late Jurassic scene.*

Chinese flocks

A remarkable find in China in 1996 may shed some light on the evolution of *Archaeopteryx. Sinosauropteryx* was found in rocks that are 120 million years old. It was slightly smaller than a chicken and had distinct traces of downy filaments up to 4 cm long all over its body. These proto-feathers may have originally evolved for insulation.

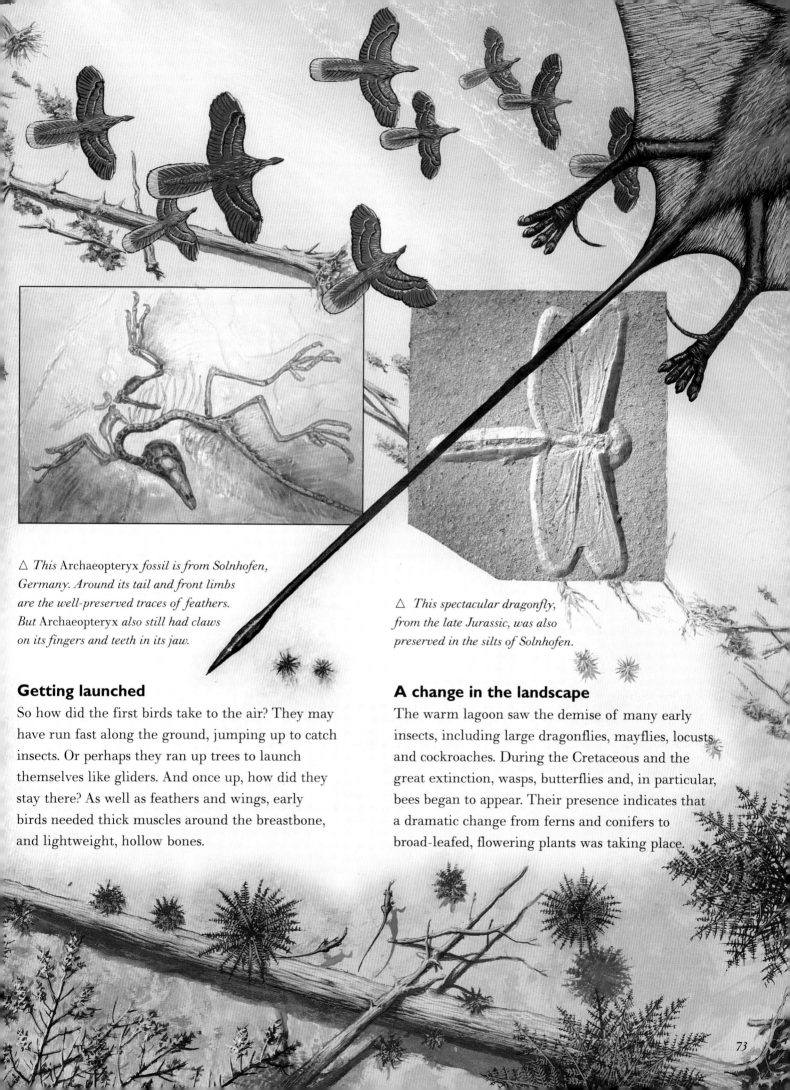

△ *This* Archaeopteryx *fossil is from Solnhofen, Germany. Around its tail and front limbs are the well-preserved traces of feathers. But* Archaeopteryx *also still had claws on its fingers and teeth in its jaw.*

△ *This spectacular dragonfly, from the late Jurassic, was also preserved in the silts of Solnhofen.*

Getting launched

So how did the first birds take to the air? They may have run fast along the ground, jumping up to catch insects. Or perhaps they ran up trees to launch themselves like gliders. And once up, how did they stay there? As well as feathers and wings, early birds needed thick muscles around the breastbone, and lightweight, hollow bones.

A change in the landscape

The warm lagoon saw the demise of many early insects, including large dragonflies, mayflies, locusts and cockroaches. During the Cretaceous and the great extinction, wasps, butterflies and, in particular, bees began to appear. Their presence indicates that a dramatic change from ferns and conifers to broad-leafed, flowering plants was taking place.

Creatures of the Ice

Any creature that survived the cataclysmic events at the end of the Cretaceous lived in a time of great opportunity. All the large predators and herbivores had been wiped off the face of the Earth. The remaining reptiles – lizards, snakes, turtles and small crocodiles – carried on much as they had before. However, small, adaptable creatures that had until then spent much of their lives in hiding were suddenly presented with the opportunity to inherit the Earth. This Tertiary era, the third age of life on the Earth, has been the age of the mammals and the birds.

△ *This frozen baby mammoth was recovered in 1977 from the permafrost of Siberia. Though shrunken, its internal organs and reddish hair had been preserved for more than 9,000 years. Flesh like this is so well preserved that, in the past, such finds were fed to dogs. Today, they are kept for genetic analysis.*

▽ *Woolly mammoths, woolly rhinoceroses, bears and buffalo roamed over the ice age tundra. These large creatures were well adapted for life at low temperatures, but they proved less adaptable than smaller mammals once the ice retreated.*

Survival of the fittest

Whereas birds had developed insulating feathers from the hard scales of their dinosaur ancestors, mammals grew fur from soft, porous skin. This was just as well because the world's climate grew progressively cooler over the next 50 million years. Mammalian evolution also saw experiments with size and ferocity. There were giant rhinos measuring 4 m at the shoulder and weighing 15 tonnes, and huge deer, such as the Irish elk. Sabre-tooth tigers and their marsupial equivalents lived alongside a host of other mammalian monsters, such as the woolly mammoths of Europe and the mastodons of North America.

The great freeze

Following the break-up of the supercontinent Pangaea, mammals evolved differently on each landmass. Then, 15 million years ago, an ice cap began to form on Antarctica and sea levels fell. This allowed animals to migrate between the different continents. It continued to get colder until, about 3.25 million years ago, variations in the Earth's orbit were large enough to trigger the first of a series of ice ages.

Adapt or die

As the polar regions froze, the ice reflected sunlight back into space and the Earth cooled further. When the higher latitudes cooled, equatorial regions became drier, forming the basis for the savannah grasslands and deserts of today. Though some mammals developed thick layers of fat or fur to keep warm, the changing climate led to the extinction of many species. But one group used its ingenuity to keep warm, clothing itself in the skins of others and lighting fires. These mammals were our own ancestors.

◁ *Part of the skull and the spectacular tusks of an adult woolly mammoth that roamed the tundra of England during the last ice age. This one was found in what is now part of the suburbs of London, England.*

△ *The skeleton of* Smilodon, *a sabre-tooth tiger. This powerful cat had a large head, muscular shoulders and a short tail. It was a ferocious killer, using its huge, serrated canine teeth to slash into the flesh of its prey – mostly large mammals such as mammoths and bison.*

Our Ancestors

In 1974, a group of anthropologists found fragments of bone near Hadar in Ethiopia. Before long, they had built up much of the skeleton of a young hominid (human ancestor) called *Australopithecus*, meaning southern ape. Naming her Lucy, they established that she was about three million years old. She had an ape-like skull and a small brain, but her arms were short and she could walk upright on her long legs. Since then, bones of a different *Australopithecus* have been found. These belong to a more ape-like species which had a developed skull, but longer arms and short legs.

△ *These ancient handprints were found in an Argentinian cave, along with many paintings of animals.*

△ *Flint hand axes like this were used by early humar This one was found Britain and is about 250,000 years old.*

Footprints in the sand

One day, about 3.6 million years ago, on what is now the Laetoli Plain of northern Tanzania, a layer of fresh ash from a nearby volcano was softened by a shower of rain. Three creatures wandered across it, walking upright on two legs. Two may have been holding hands, the third, smaller and younger, walked behind. Were they our ancestors?

▷ *A group of* Homo erectus, *about 1.5 million years ago, plans a hunt across the African savannah. These intelligent, early people walked upright, leaving their hands free to use tools.*

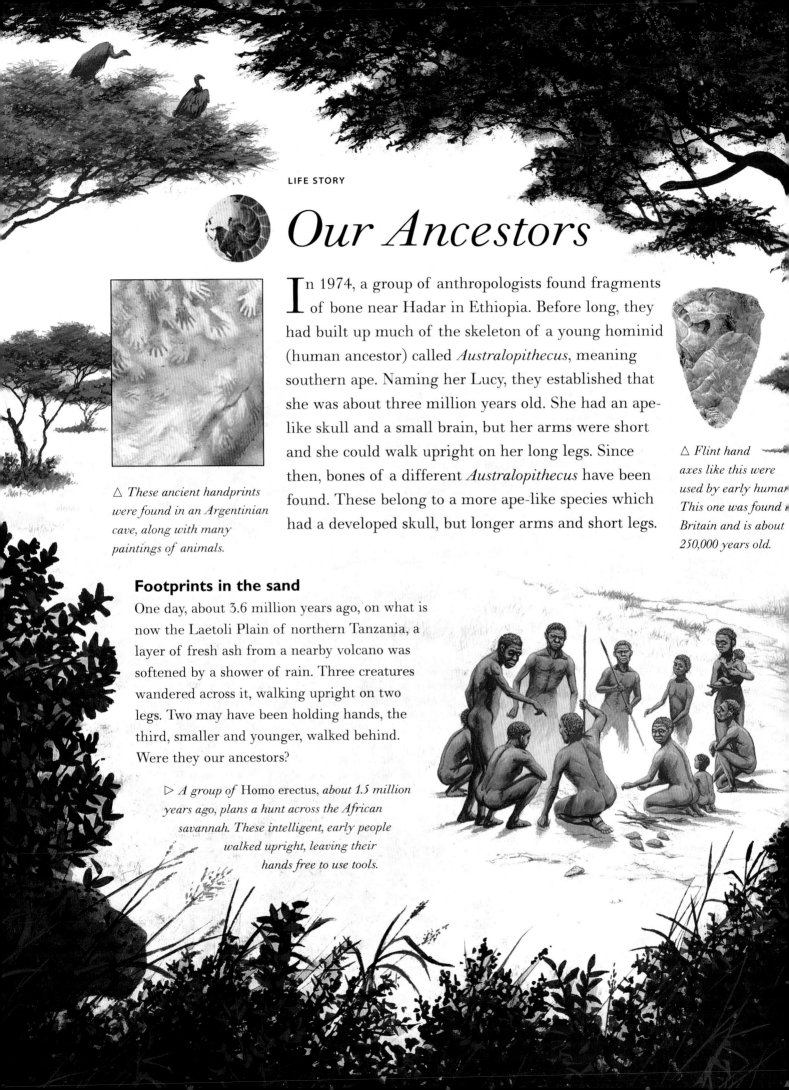

The toolmakers

In 1984, the bones of a 12-year-old boy were discovered near Lake Turkana in Kenya. They were nearly 1.5 million years old. He belonged to a species called *Homo erectus* (upright human), and was probably one of our ancestors. From about 1.8 million years ago, when *Homo erectus* evolved, the fossil sites are littered with the stone hand axes crafted by these early humans.

The road to civilization

The first people to be called *Homo sapiens* (wise human) were a tall, big-brained group that appeared in Europe about 500,000 years ago. About 200,000 years ago, another intelligent group emerged in Germany, called the Neanderthals. The first modern humans, *Homo sapiens sapiens*, emerged 40,000 years ago.

△ *These footprints, preserved in hardened volcanic ash, were left in Tanzania 3.6 million years ago, perhaps by a family of hominids. Whoever they were, they clearly walked upright. This ability may have resulted in a larger brain developing as the hands became free to manipulate tools.*

▷ *A reconstruction of the skull of* Homo erectus pekinensis *(1), an early modern human (2),* Australopithecus africanus *(3), an Australopithecine skull from between 5 million and 1.2 million years ago (4).*

Fuel from the Earth

For more than one billion years, planet Earth has teemed with life. During that time, living organisms have trapped the Sun's energy and stored it in the chemicals of their bodies. Much of that chemical energy is now stored underground as fossil fuels – coal, gas and oil. Today, we are releasing that trapped solar energy by burning the fuels, and putting the carbon they contain back into the atmosphere as carbon dioxide. The fuels provide us with energy to fire our power stations and generate electricity. They give us fuel for cars and aircraft, and they provide most of the raw materials for making plastics, artificial fibres and a host of other chemicals.

△ Oil is not always found where it is needed. The trans-Alaskan pipeline carries oil 1,284 km across the Arctic.

▽ This nuclear power station at Sizewell in Suffolk, England, is powered by uranium. Only a tiny quantity of fuel is required, but the radioactive waste it produces is difficult and expensive to handle safely.

Fossil forests

During the Carboniferous period 300 million years ago, vast forests covered much of the Earth's land surface. Giant tree ferns and cycads grew, died and decomposed. Where they fell in swampy ground, there was not enough oxygen for them to rot and they turned into thick layers of peat. Sometimes, sea levels rose and covered the remains with layers of sand or shale. As it was buried deeper and deeper, the peat was compressed into coal.

Oil and gas

Many of the great multitude of creatures that live in the oceans are eaten or decomposed by bacteria. However, some sink into oxygen-poor waters and become buried in the sediments. The abundant bacteria that live hundreds of metres beneath the sea floor survive off these organic remains and slowly convert them into oil and methane gas.

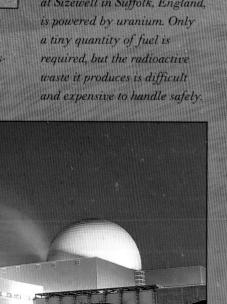

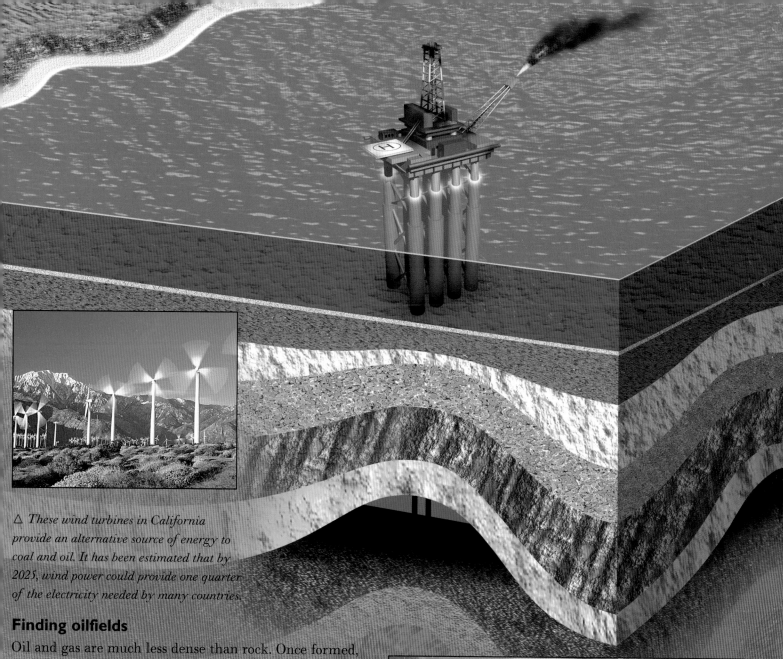

△ *These wind turbines in California provide an alternative source of energy to coal and oil. It has been estimated that by 2025, wind power could provide one quarter of the electricity needed by many countries.*

Finding oilfields

Oil and gas are much less dense than rock. Once formed, they tend to rise up through porous rocks until they can go no further. Oil prospectors searching for the 'black gold' begin by looking for the sort of geological formations that will trap it. The oil and gas themselves fill the tiny spaces within rocks such as sandstone. Where rocks of the right age are overlaid by domes of impervious rocks such as clay or salt, huge reservoirs of oil and gas may collect.

Oil strike!

One hundred years ago, shallow oil wells would often produce a gush of oil under natural pressure. Today, the technology to extract oil has become complex and expensive. Pumping out the oil only extracts a fraction of what is there. Seawater and chemical solvents help extract more. Even so, at the present rate, the oil will only last a few decades; the coal and gas a little longer.

△ *Sometime in the future, the coal and oil will run out, but the Sun will continue to shine. Banks of reflecting dishes such as these in Australia are already used to concentrate the Sun's energy and generate electrical power.*

Metals from the Earth

The Earth was formed from raw ingredients originally cooked up inside stars and spewed out into space. Processes inside the planet have concentrated these elements, such as metals, in quantities useful to humans. The minerals that contain these concentrated elements are called ores. Some minerals are carried along cracks and fissures in rock when molten igneous rocks rise through the crust. Other minerals are deposited in crystalline veins as heat drives off water containing dissolved minerals. Some of the richest mines of copper, lead, zinc and gold are formed in this way.

△ When hot fluids containing dissolved minerals fill a cavity in a rock, they form a geode. First, silica is deposited, then as the cavity fills, larger quartz crystals grow, often coloured by trace metals.

Extracting metals

Few metals occur in their pure form in nature. Gold is a notable exception. Most metallic minerals are chemical compounds with very different properties to the metals they contain. The process of smelting is used to extract the metal from the ore. Both heat and a reducing agent, such as carbon in the form of charcoal, are used to pull the metal's chemical companions away from it.

▽ Useful minerals are often deposited around hot, igneous rock. Water, saturated in dissolved minerals, is driven outwards by the heat.

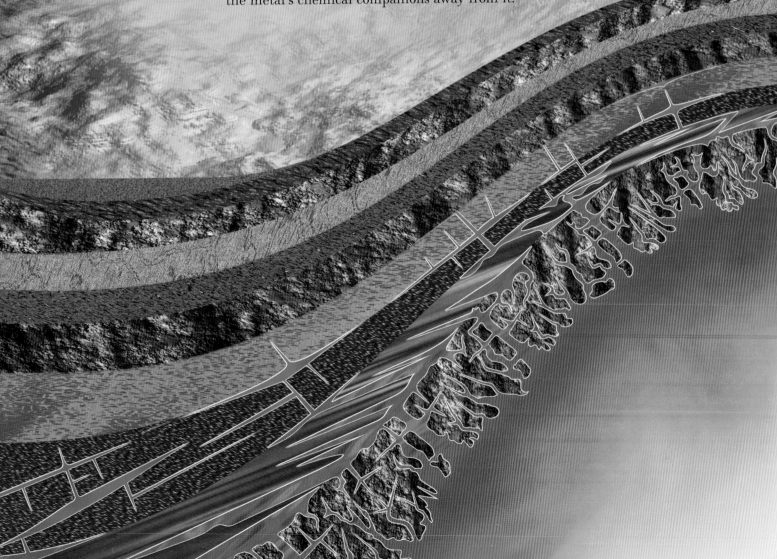

◁ *Protected by heat resistant clothes, a worker takes a sample of molten iron from a blast furnace. Inside the furnace, hot air fans the flames through a mixture of iron ore, coke and limestone. Once the waste, or slag, is skimmed off, the molten iron is cast into ingots.*

The other side

Despite the value of the metals they produce, mines have also left a legacy of pollution and damage. For every tonne of ore extracted, there can be thousands of tonnes of waste rock spilled across the hillside. Sometimes, the waste rocks contain poisons that kill the surrounding trees. Artificial dams burst, mines flood and tanks leak, washing mud, debris and toxic chemicals down rivers. In some cases, the mines are located in environmentally sensitive areas or in populated territories.

Holes in the ground

Mining techniques depend on the concentration of the ore, its depth and its value. Where ore lies in a thick vein underground, tunnels and shafts can be sunk. Sometimes there is a large body of less concentrated ore near the surface and it can be dug out from an opencast pit. Sometimes nature has already done the digging. Deposits of gold, for example, are concentrated in river gravels.

Future prospects

As mines on the land become exhausted, we will need to look elsewhere. There are potentially rich sources in the ocean. Some areas of the ocean floor are littered with manganese nodules and other rare metals. However, they lie at great depths and are in international waters. One day, mining might happen in space. A single small asteroid, towed back to the Earth, could provide many of the valuable metals that the world needs for centuries.

▽ *Once the rock cools, the minerals are left in cracks and fissures, forming metal-rich veins. Miners cut shafts and galleries underground to reach the veins.*

▽ *This great opencast mine in New Mexico, US, is one of the largest artificial holes on the planet.*

◁ Lapis lazuli is a complex sodium aluminium silicate. This semi-precious stone is formed in igneous and metamorphic rocks that are rich in carbonate.

Gems from the Deep

Any stone or crystal worn as jewellery can be regarded as a gem. Some are organic in origin, such as amber (fossilized tree resin), jet (hard, black coal), opal (silicified wood) and pearl (shell). Many other semi-precious stones are silicate minerals such as quartz (rock crystal), amethyst, jade, garnet and topaz. The most precious stones are also the rarest and the most durable – ruby, sapphire, emerald and diamond. These mineral gems are formed under particular conditions of pressure and temperature, deep in the Earth's mantle. It is only later that they are thrown up to the surface.

▽ For centuries, the prospect of great wealth led alchemists to try to convert base materials into gold and gems. We know now that they could never have succeeded.

△ Natural diamond crystal is found embedded in volcanic kimberlite rock. This type of rock is named after the area in which it is found – Kimberley, South Africa.

▽ Carbon is dragged down from the Earth's surface to the upper mantle, where the pressure transforms it into diamond.

Humble beginnings

The tightly packed crystal structure of diamond makes it the hardest natural substance on the Earth. Yet, it is made of carbon, the same element that makes pencil lead or soot. Where this carbon came from is uncertain. Perhaps it was once limestone, coal or even a carbon-rich meteorite (*see below, illustration 1*) and was then pulled into the Earth's mantle on a slab of old ocean crust (*2*).

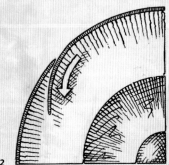

◁ *Quartz is a form of silica. This quartz crystal was photographed using coloured light. Flaws in the quartz catch the light, making it shimmer.*

△ *Rutilated quartz contains needle-like crystals of rutile, an ore of titanium.*

The birth of a diamond

Over millions of years and at about 600 kilometres beneath the Earth's surface, the carbon was slowly transformed into a diamond. However, its rise to the surface would have been much more rapid. This is because it must have been ejected in the type of volcano, now mercifully extinct, which erupted at supersonic speeds (*3*).

Many facets

A rough natural diamond has eight sides (*4*). To give it its sparkle, the surface must be carefully cut so that it has many facets (*5*). The best-known diamond cut is called a brilliant and has 58 facets, making it especially sparkly. As well as adorning jewellery, diamonds can also be used in the blades of delicate saws or in drill bits.

△ *These two uncut diamonds are shown in their natural state, after being dug from the Oranjemund mines in Namibia.*

△ *A cut, polished diamond may be worth several thousand dollars per carat. One carat is 0.2 grammes.*

Emerald alchemy

Emeralds usually form in hot granite when scaldingly hot fluids containing beryllium and chromium react with carborundum or aluminium oxide. However, some of the most beautiful emeralds are from Colombia and seem to have formed when highly pressurized hot water dissolved salt and gypsum from sedimentary rocks which then reacted with clay minerals in the surrounding shale.

3

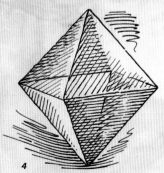

4

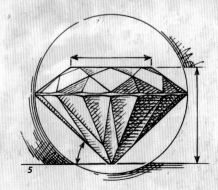

5

Human Creators

In the four billion years since the heavy bombardment of the Earth ceased, continents have split and collided, oceans have opened and vanished, mountain ranges have grown, then eroded away. But never has change been faster or more spectacular than over the past few thousand years. The recent transformation of the planet is mostly due to the activities of a single species, *Homo sapiens sapiens* – ourselves. It is hard to imagine what the world would be like without human beings. Since ancient times, we have built and burrowed, chopped and changed – taming the landscape to suit our needs. The concrete jungles and cultivated landscapes are clear evidence that we have become the rulers of the surface of the Earth and all the species upon it. We are the creators and the destroyers of wonders.

△ *Though now surrounded by jungle, the great Mayan pyramids of Tikal in Guatemala are impressive examples of human creativity.*

A new garden of Eden

Look down at the surface of the Earth from a plane, or even from space, and the patterns are striking. For hundreds of kilometres, parts of the Earth are a patchwork of fields, outlined by the unnaturally straight lines of roads and fences. It is even possible to see political and economic boundaries, as different agricultural policies meet along lines that seem to be drawn with a ruler.

◁ *Powerful people of every era have tried to leave enduring monuments to their life and times. These giant faces of American presidents are carved out of the natural rock of Mount Rushmore in South Dakota, US.*

Protecting and preserving

Many regions of wilderness do still remain on the planet, complete with a rich biodiversity of plants and animals. Work is in progress to preserve these areas and to prevent further pollution and destruction. We have also taken it upon ourselves to try to protect individual species, or at least the ones we have identified. Huge efforts are going into the preservation of rare animals such as the giant panda of China or the California condor.

The wonders of the world

Not all human industry is destructive – we have created some works of great beauty and benefit too. Which ones qualify as the wonders of our civilization is a matter of individual taste. Maybe they are the great buildings of our modern age. Perhaps they are products of science, such as space rockets and suspension bridges. They could even be on a smaller scale – a painting, a piece of music, a book or a garden in full bloom.

A web of knowledge

One of the greatest human achievements is the quest for knowledge and understanding. We have explored our planet's surface and journeyed into space. We are discovering the secrets of science and the mysteries of our own bodies. No one person can contain all this knowledge, but through our libraries and communications networks, we have spun a web of knowledge around the planet that people can access. It brings a potential far greater than that of any individual.

△ *Great buildings, ingenious structures and powerful machines keep our economies thriving and our lives moving. But some human creations are designed to fulfil our spiritual needs, while others are simply for pleasure or amazement.*

Human Destroyers

Life on the Earth may be facing an even greater crisis than the mass extinctions of the past. For the last three hundred years, vertebrate species have been disappearing at an average of one per year, and today more than 3,500 animal species are under threat. Plants, fungi and micro-organisms are also vanishing. If the present trend continues, it has been estimated that at least one quarter of all living creatures will disappear before the human population levels out in about 50 years' time. The reasons for current losses are hunting, competition from introduced species and, in particular, loss of habitats.

△ *Untreated waste pours into the sea from an outflow pipe on the English coast. Untreated sewage can cause blooms of algae which use up oxygen from the water. Chemicals can poison life directly.*

◁ *Despite improved techniques for dealing with oil spills, it can take many years for an area to recover from a major spill.*

Lost worlds

Humans have been changing the landscape since the ice ages. With the invention of the flint hand-axe, the systematic felling of the forests of much of northern Europe began. In Australia, the telltale signs of charcoal show that the first human settlers arrived 40,000 to 50,000 years ago, and this coincides with the extinction of large birds and marsupials on that continent. Today, about 1% of the world's 17 million square kilometres of tropical rainforest is cleared every year. This also releases huge quantities of carbon dioxide into the atmosphere.

Polluted planet

Six billion people produce a lot of waste, much of which is dumped with little or no treatment. We live in an industrialized world that requires the manufacture, use and transport of concentrated chemicals and even radioactive materials. It is often the case that laws are broken, not enforced or non-existent, and the land, rivers and seas suffer as a result.

▷ *A stricken oil tanker floats helplessly in the sea, its precious cargo spilling out to clog beaches and poison wildlife.*

Danger for humankind

What about the idea of Gaia (named after the Earth goddess), that our planet acts like a single organism to keep conditions favourable for life? Does that mean that we can leave nature to clean up the mess? Professor James Lovelock, who introduced the concept of Gaia, does not doubt that this theory is correct – but he has never claimed that it will operate in favour of one species, least of all humankind.

Islands of hope

In the sea of destruction, there are islands of hope. In the 1870s, with the Industrial Revolution well underway, the world's first national park was established – Yellowstone, in Wyoming, US. Today, there are more than 3,000 national parks and wildlife reserves, covering more than four million square kilometres of the world. And perhaps the invention of space flight has come just in time. Not for us to evacuate, but for us to recognize the need to protect our planet. From space, polluted rivers, forest fires and deserts are clearly visible, national boundaries fade away.

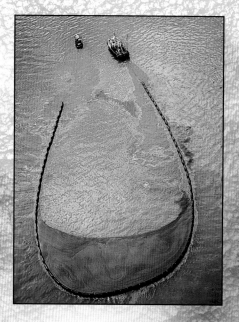

△ *After the oil tanker* Sea Empress *ran aground off the coast of South Wales in 1996, trawlers towed floating booms to try to contain the oil slicks and prevent them from drifting onto beaches.*

◁ *During the Gulf War in 1991, many Kuwaiti oil wells were left blazing. The thick palls of smoke travelled hundreds of kilometres and were clearly visible from space.*

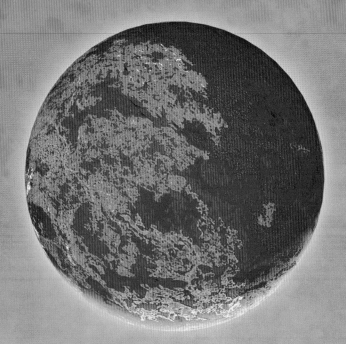

◁▽ *Several billion years into the future and the Earth and Moon have been scorched to cinders. The Sun is expanding into a red giant and has boiled away the oceans and atmosphere. Planet Earth is no longer the blue and green jewel that we once called home.*

The End of the Earth

The Earth has been our home for about half a million years, and home to life in some form for most of its 4.5 billion years. But as we have discovered, the Earth is a dynamic and active planet. Volcanoes erupt, continents split in two, mountains rise up, even rock is not steady. One day, the radioactive heat sources that fuel such changes will decay, the molten outer core will freeze and the Earth will be nothing more than a dead ember floating in space. However, more immediately, our planet is under constant threat from outside and even from ourselves.

▷ *Whatever the cause, we can be sure that one day the Earth will not be as hospitable as it is now. If human life is to survive, we will have to find ourselves a new home elsewhere in the Universe.*

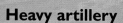

Heavy artillery

The Earth has been under more or less regular bombardment since its birth. The early impacts were huge, probably melting the entire surface. Though their size and frequency have lessened, they have not stopped. Comets and asteroids have caused mass extinctions in the past, and unless we can deflect them, they will almost certainly do so again. But even if there is a major impact, past evidence suggests that life will not only survive but make the most of a catastrophe.

Cosmic roasting

Space is a dangerous place for a small planet. Old massive stars, our Sun's neighbours, could explode as supernovae in a thermonucleur fireball. This would damage the Earth's ozone layer and affect life, but probably not destroy it altogether. Similarly, the gamma ray burst released in a collision between two neutron stars would blast the Earth with radiation, roasting it as it turns, like a chicken on a spit. But again, the damage would probably not be terminal.

The human threat

Could we destroy our planet by our own actions?
With the powers that we have today, the answer is,
probably not. For all the devastation they cause, nuclear
weapons are no match for explosive volcanoes and
asteroid impacts. Maybe our activities will change the
climate, damage the ozone layer or release dangerous
new organisms and chemicals into the environment.
The results would indeed be terrible, but life is resilient.
Somehow the world would survive, with or without us.

The end of the Sun

When time does run out for the Earth, it will probably
be because the hydrogen at the heart of our Sun has
been exhausted. As the Sun dies, it will begin to swell
into a bloated red giant. Then, over a few thousand years,
it will engulf the Earth and scorch away the atmosphere,
oceans and, eventually, all life. But there is no need to
worry quite yet. It will be another four or five billion
years before this catastrophic event happens, and by
then, we should be well on our way to the stars.

△ *The last of a series of giant spacecraft pulls
away from Earth orbit and leaves to colonize
new worlds. Constructed out of an asteroid, the
craft, named* Utopia, *carries a complete sample
of life on the Earth – land, sea, plants and
animals, as well as the last 1,000 human
descendants. Our planet is dead, but life goes on.*

Earth Facts

PLANETARY DATA

Equatorial diameter	12,756 km
Volume	1.084×10^{12} km³
Mass	5.9742×10^{24} kg
Density	5.52 of water
Surface gravity	9.78 ms⁻²
Day length	23.9345 hours
Year length	365.256 days
Axial inclination	23.44°
Age	4,700 million years approx.
Distance from the Sun	Min. 147 million km
	Max. 152 million km
Surface area	509.6 million km²
Land surface	148 million km²
Oceans cover	71% of surface
Atmosphere	Nitrogen 78%, Oxygen 21%, other 1%
Av. height of land	840 m above sea level
Av. depth of ocean	3,808 m
Continental crust	35 km av. thick
Oceanic crust	7 km av. thick
Lithosphere	75 km deep
Mantle	2,900 km thick
Outer core	2,200 km thick
Inner core	1,200 km thick

MAJOR EARTHQUAKES

Location	Year	Magnitude	Deaths
China (Zhangbei)	1998	6.2	50
Afghanistan	1998	6.1	4,000
N. Iran	1997	7.1	1,560
Russia (Sakhalin)	1995	7.5	2,000
Japan (Kobe)	1995	7.2	6,310
S. California	1994	6.8	60
S. India (Osmanabad)	1993	6.4	9,748
Philippines	1990	7.7	1,653
NW. Iran	1990	7.5	36,000
San Francisco	1989	6.9	275
Armenia	1988	7.0	25,000
Mexico City	1985	8.1	7,200
N. Yemen	1982	6.0	2,800
S. Italy	1980	7.2	4,500
NE. Iran	1978	7.7	25,000
Tangshan, China	1976	8.2	242,000
Guatemala City	1976	7.5	22,778
NE. Iran	1968	7.4	11,600
Nan-shan, China	1927	8.3	200,000
Japan	1923	8.3	143,000
Gansu, China	1920	8.6	180,000
Messina, Italy	1908	7.5	120,000
San Francisco	1906	8.3	500
Calcutta, India	1737	-	300,000
Hokkaido, Japan	1730	-	137,000
Shensi, China	1556	-	830,000
Antioch, Turkey	526	-	250,000

PROPERTIES OF COMMON MINERALS

Name	Type	Hardness	Crystal	Optical
Talc	Silicate	1	Cubic	Pale green or grey; pearly lustre
Graphite	Element	1-2	Trigonal	Grey metallic lustre
Gypsum	Sulphate	2	Monoclinic	White to transparent
Calcite	Carbonate	3	Trigonal/ Hexagonal	Double refraction
Barytes	Sulphate	3-3.5	Orthorhombic	Pale, translucent
Fluorite	Halide	4	Cubic	Many colours, fluorescent
Pyrite	Sulphide	6-6.5	Cubic	Commonly known as "fool's gold"
Quartz	Oxide	7	Trigonal/Hexagonal	Translucent
Garnet	Silicate	7	Cubic	Various forms, often plum red
Tourmaline	Silicate	7-7.5	Trigonal/Hexagonal	Pink and green
Zircon	Silicate	7.5	Tetragonal	Often brown
Beryl	Silicate	7-8	Trigonal/Hexagonal	Many colours, emerald green
Spinel	Oxide	7.5-8	Cubic	Many colours
Corundum	Oxide	9	Trigonal/Hexagonal	Various forms incl. ruby & sapphire
Diamond	Element	10	Cubic	Transparent, sparkles if cut

A mineral's optical properties include not only its colour but also its transparency and lustre, or shine. Hardness is a scale based on ten minerals. These range from talc, the softest (1) to diamond, the hardest (10).

MAJOR VOLCANOES

Name	Ht(m)	Major eruptions	Last
Bezymyannaya, Russia	2,800	1955-56	1984
El Chichón, Mexico	1,349	1982	1982
Erebus, Antarctica	4,023	1947, 1972	1986
Mt Etna, Italy	3,236	Frequent	1991
Fuji, Japan	3,776	1707	1707
Hekla, Iceland	1,491	1693, 1845, 1947-48, 1970	1981
Helgafell, Iceland	215	1973	1973
Kiluea, Hawaii	1,247	Frequent	1991
Klyuchevskoy, Russia	4,850	1700-1966, 1984	1985
Krakatoa, Sumatra	818	Frequent, esp. 1883	1980
La Soufrière, St Vincent	1,232	1718, 1812, 1902, 1971-72	1979
Mauna Loa, Hawaii	4,172	Frequent	1984
Soufrière Hills, Montserrat	915	1995	1998
Nyamaragira, Zaire	3,056	1921-38, 1971, 1980	1984
Paricutin, Mexico	3,188	1943-52	1952
Mt Pelée, Martinique	1,397	1902, 1929-32	1932
Pinatubo, Philippines	1,462	1391, 1991	1991
Popocatepetl, Mexico	5,483	1920	1943
Mt Rainier, US	4,392	1st century BC, 1820	1882
Ruapehu, N.Zealand	2,796	1945, 1953, 1969, 1975	1986
Mt St Helens, US	2,549	Frequent, esp. 1980	1987
Santorini, Greece	1,315	Frequent, esp. 1470BC	1950
Stromboli, Italy	931	Frequent	1986
Surtsey, Iceland	174	1963-67	1967
Unzen, Japan	1,360	1360, 1791	1991
Mt Vesuvius, Italy	1,289	Frequent, esp. AD79	1944

PRINCIPAL ORE MINERALS

Ore of	Mineral	Composition	Features
Aluminium	Cryolite	Na_3AlF_6	White, extracted by electrolysis
Copper	Chalcopyrite	Sulphide	Brassy yellow
	Cuprite	Oxide	Black
	Malachite	Carbonate	Green
Gold	Native	Metal	Golden
Iron	Pyrite	Sulphide	Brassy yellow
	Magnetite	Oxide	Black
	Hematite	Hematite	Black/reddish
	Siderite	Carbonate	Orange
Lead	Galena	Sulphide	Metallic black
Silver	Native	Metal	Silver
Tin	Cassiterite	Oxide	Black/brown
Titanium	Ilmenite	Oxide	Black opaque
Uranium	Uraninite	Oxide	Dull brown/black
Zinc	Sphalerite	Sulphide	Black

GEOLOGICAL TIMELINE

Mya		Era
21	Quaternary	Cenozoic
	Pliocene	
	Miocene	
	Oligocene	
65	Paleocene and Eocene	
135	Cretaceous	Mesozoic
195	Jurassic	
225	Triassic	
280	Permian	
345	Carboniferous	Paleozoic
395	Devonian	
430	Silurian	
500	Ordovician	
570	Cambrian	
Mya	Precambrian	

Mya stands for Millions of years ago.

The changing fossil record (above) provides an effective means of dating rocks. So-called zone or index fossils have been picked as key markers for each time. The fossil record goes back to the Precambrian era which began 600 million years ago.

Glossary

Ash The name given to the fine, powdery material which is blown out by gas during a volcanic eruption. Ash can spread for thousands of kilometres and fall like snow to form layers many centimetres thick.

Asteroid A rocky object, anything from a few metres to a few hundred kilometres across, in orbit around the Sun. Most asteroids are in the asteroid belt between the orbits of Mars and Jupiter, but some come in to the inner Solar System and, every million years or so, one collides with the Earth.

Atmosphere The thin layer of air, composed mostly of nitrogen and oxygen, that is held in place around the Earth by gravity.

Atom The smallest component of an element that retains its chemical properties. Even the biggest atom is only half a millionth of a millimetre across.

Aurora The display of what look like coloured curtains of light at high latitudes, caused by energetic particles from the Sun streaming in towards the Earth's magnetic poles and striking atoms in the atmosphere.

Basalt One of the commonest rocks in the Earth's crust. It is created by partial melting of the mantle and erupts as a runny lava from volcanoes. It is dark, dense and fine-grained.

Biodiversity The full range of plant, animal and micro-organism species found in a particular habitat. The health of an ecosystem can be measured by the degree of its diversity.

Canyon A deep valley or gorge, often with near vertical sides. A canyon is carved by a river running through an arid, mountainous region.

CFC Chlorofluorocarbons are the chemicals which once were widely used in aerosol sprays, fire extinguishers and refrigerators and which, when released into the atmosphere, damage the ozone layer. Their use is now strictly limited by international agreement.

Continent Great land mass on the surface of the Earth. There are seven continents.

Core The innermost 7,000 kilometres of our planet, composed mostly of iron with traces of nickel and other minerals. The central 2,400 kilometres is solid, but the outer core is molten and slowly circulating. Electrical currents within the core generate the planet's magnetic field.

Crater A circular structure on the surface of the Earth or other body caused either by a volcanic eruption from underneath or by an impact from above.

Cretaceous The geological period between 135 and 65 million years ago. Life flourished during this warm period. The period ended suddenly with the extinction of the dinosaurs and many other species.

Crust The comparatively thin skin of rock that covers the surface of the Earth. Beneath the oceans it is only about 7 km thick, but in continents it averages 35 km.

Crystal A substance in which the atoms or molecules are bound in an orderly three-dimensional pattern. Different materials have different but characteristic crystal shapes. Many minerals are found as natural crystals.

Desert An area in which the climate is very dry.

DNA Deoxyribonucleic acid is the chemical which carries the genetic code of life. It is made up of a long chain that forms a double helix or spiral structure.

Earthquake An often violent shaking of the Earth caused when two of the plates that make up the Earth's crust crack as they scrape past one another. Earthquakes are most frequent along plate boundaries.

Ecosystem A natural habitat with all the interdependent species that live within it. Without outside interference, an ecosystem will flourish unchanged for long periods.

El Niño The South American name given to the warm ocean current that occasionally flows towards the coast of Peru, disrupting fisheries and wildlife and bringing droughts to some parts of the world and storms and floods to others.

Epicentre The point on the Earth's surface directly above the focus of an earthquake, the place where the ground cracks.

Erosion The process by which rocks are worn away, usually as a result of the action of water, wind or ice.

Estuary The place where a river widens and slows as it flows out into the sea. As the water slows, it can deposit the sediments it is carrying to form a delta.

Fault A crack in the Earth's crust that forms during an earthquake as a result of stresses within the rock.

Fold A region of rocks that have been deformed or bent by movements in the Earth's crust.

Fossil The traces of a prehistoric plant or animal preserved within rocks or sediments. Fossils can be made up of the original hard parts of the organism or they can be replaced by other minerals.

Fossil fuel Fossil fuels include coal, oil and natural gas, all produced from the decay, burial and fossilization of organic remains. Fossil fuels have taken millions of years to form, but humans have almost exhausted them in just a few centuries.

Glacier Literally, a river of ice that builds up in a mountain valley as a result of the compression of snow. Although the ice seems solid, a glacier can flow slowly downhill, gouging out a deep U-shaped valley.

Global warming A general warming of the Earth's climate brought about by increasing levels of so-called greenhouse gases such as carbon dioxide in the atmosphere. It is predicted that human activity will result in global warming of several degrees over the next century.

Gondwanaland The name given to the great southern continent that resulted from the break up of the supercontinent Pangaea. It included present day Africa, South America, Australia, Antarctica and India.

Granite A crystalline igneous rock produced by the upwelling, or intrusion, of molten crustal rocks. It contains the minerals quartz, mica and feldspar.

Gravity Gravity is the force that makes objects attract one another. It holds us on the surface of the Earth, keeps the Moon in orbit around our planet and the Earth in orbit around the Sun.

Greenhouse effect The greenhouse effect is caused by gases such as water vapour and carbon dioxide in the atmosphere which allow sunlight into the Earth's surface but prevent the escape of heat. As a result, the gases act like a blanket, keeping the planet warm in the same way as the glass in a greenhouse keeps plants inside warm.

Hot spot A hot spot is a place on the surface of the Earth above an upwelling plume of hot mantle material. Hot spots are often the site of intensive long-term volcanic activity. Examples include Hawaii and Iceland.

Hydrothermal vent Where volcanic forces rise beneath the ocean crust, for example along the mid-ocean ridges, they can heat groundwater so that it jets out of underwater springs or vents.

Ice age An ice age is a prolonged period during which the Earth's climate cools and ice sheets and glaciers spread from the poles. It may be triggered by periodic variations in the Earth's orbit around the Sun. There have been four ice ages in the last two million years and there may be more to come.

Igneous Igneous rocks are produced by the melting of material deep within the Earth's crust or upper mantle. They are of two main types – extrusive igneous rocks which come out of volcanoes and cool quickly, so they are usually fine-grained, and intrusive igneous rocks which bulge up in large masses within a continent. They cool more slowly and as a result are sometimes crystalline.

Laurasia The great northern continent formed from the break up, 200 million years ago, of the supercontinent Pangaea. It was made up of present-day Europe, North America, Greenland and Asia.

Lava The molten rock which flows out of a volcano and then solidifies.

Magma Molten rock within the Earth. Sometimes it rises within a volcano to flow out as lava.

Magnetometer A highly sensitive instrument used by geologists to measure the Earth's magnetic field.

Magnetosphere The magnetic bubble formed around the Earth by the planet's magnetic field. It protects us from high-energy charged particles that stream out from the Sun.

Mantle The thick layer of dense silicate rocks that forms the bulk of the Earth beneath the thin crust and above the iron core. Although virtually solid, it carries heat from the interior of the planet and produces volcanic activity on the surface.

Metamorphic Metamorphic rocks are rocks which have been changed by heat and pressure. They can be derived from either igneous or sedimentary rocks. The heat and pressure can turn shale into slate, limestone into marble and sandstone into quartzite.

Mid-ocean ridge The long range of underwater mountains that runs down the centres of many of the world's oceans. It forms lines of undersea volcanoes from which new ocean crust is spreading.

Mineral A naturally formed chemical substance with a precise molecular structure. Minerals are the building blocks of rocks.

Moraine The lines and piles of stones and mud deposited along the sides and at the end of a glacier.

Ore A mineral rich in a particular useful substance such as a metal, and used in commercial quantities for producing that material.

Ozone A form of oxygen molecule that contains three oxygen atoms. It forms naturally in a thin layer in the stratosphere, about 20 kilometres above us, where it filters out potentially damaging ultraviolet radiation from sunlight. However, it is destroyed by chemicals such as CFCs.

Pangaea The supercontinent containing all the world's land masses. It existed between about 250 and 200 million years ago and broke up to form Gondwanaland and Laurasia, with the Tethys Ocean in between them.

Permian The geological period between about 280 and 225 million years ago. Some of the first large reptiles lived during the Permian period. However, it ended abruptly with the extinction of many species.

Pillow lava Deposits of volcanic lava shaped like a series of pillows. They erupted underwater and were quickly quenched and solidified by the water before they could flow far.

Plate A unit of the rocky lithosphere – the crust and hard top to the mantle – that can slide intact over the Earth's surface as a result of continental drift.

Pyroclastic flow A deadly flow of volcanic lava, ash, super-heated steam and gas that can race downhill from a volcanic eruption, scorching everything in its path.

Rift A valley created by a pair of faults or cracks with the land in between subsiding. It is often a sign that a continent is being stretched apart. The Great Rift Valley in East Africa is a good example.

Sedimentary Sedimentary rocks are rocks laid down, usually in layers, by water or by wind, ice and vegetation. They are mostly formed from the erosion of other rocks, and these so-called clastic rocks include shale and sandstone. Others are chemical deposits such as limestone and gypsum.

Seismic wave A wave running through the Earth usually produced by an earthquake, though explosions can also trigger a seismic wave.

Seismograph An instrument for measuring seismic waves.

Silicate One of the group of minerals containing silicon and oxygen atoms bound to other elements such as metals. Silicates are the main rock-forming minerals of the planet.

Smelting The process in which an ore is heated to extract a metal from it.

Stalactite A deposit of calcium carbonate hanging like an icicle from the roof of a cave.

Stalagmite A column of calcium carbonate rising up from a cave floor, often beneath a stalactite and formed by a similar process.

Subduction The process by which old, dense ocean crust descends back into the Earth's mantle.

Tornado A small but extremely violent storm in which a funnel-shaped column of cloud rotates rapidly as warm air rises within it. Tornadoes can reach speeds of several hundred kilometres per hour and are common in parts of the US and Australia.

Tsunami Sometimes known as a tidal wave, a tsunami can be triggered by an underwater earthquake or landslide. In open ocean it may be only a few centimetres high, but it can travel great distances, and as it reaches the shore, can build into a destructive wall of water tens of metres high.

Vertebrate An animal with a backbone. Vertebrate species include fish, amphibians reptiles, birds and mammals as well as humans.

Volcano A place where molten magma rises to the surface of the planet and is released, often with violent results. A volcano can build into a mountain thousands of metres high.

Index

Acknowledgements

The publishers would like to thank the following illustrators:
Julian Baker 15 *cr*, 16 *l*, 18 *cr*, 20 *bl*, 25 *tr*, 26 *tr*, 29 *cl*, 30 *br*, 32 *cl*, 35 *cl*, 35 *t (icons)*, 36 *tr*, 39 *r*, 40 *cl*, 47 *tr*, 49 *tr*, 62 *c*; **Julian Baum** 10–11, 16–17, 26–27, 54–55, 86–87, 88–89; **Tim Duke** 12–13, 14–15, 19, 20–21, 24–25, 38–39, 50–51, 78–79, 80–81; **James Field** 60–61, 64–65, 66–67, 68–69, 70–71, 72–73, 74–75, 76–77; **Gary Hincks** 11 *tr*, 37 *r*, 56–57 *(line drawings)*, 82–83 *(line drawings)*; **Richard Holloway** 22–23, 32–33, 40–41, 52–53; **Mark Preston** *(digital montages)* 6–7, 8–9, 30–31, 34–35, 36–37, 42–43, 46–47, 48–49, 56–57, 58–59, 82–83, 84–85, icons.

The publishers would like to thank the following for supplying photographs:

Front cover *t* Science Photo Library/Keith Kent, *tr* Science Photo Library/Kent Wood, *cl* Science Photo Library/John Mead, *c* Tony Stone Images/Earth Imaging, *cr* Science Photo Library/Explorer/Krafft, *bl* Science Photo Library/Noboru Komine, *bc* Science Photo Library/Phil Jude, *br* Pictor International Ltd, **Back cover** *bl* Planet Earth Pictures/Krafft – I+V, *cl* SPL/Vaughan Fleming, **end papers:** The Bridgeman Art Library/British Library, London, UK

3 *cl* Planet Earth Pictures/J.P.Nacivet, *bc* Tony Stone Images/Frans Lanting, 4-5 *t* NHPA/Roger Tidman, 6 *tl* The Bridgeman Art Library/Bible Society, London, *c* Science Photo Library/ESA, *cr* Planet Earth Pictures, 6-7 *b* The Bridgeman Art Library/Vatican Museum & Galleries, Rome, 7 *b* The Bridgeman Art Library/San Marco, Venice/Francesco Turino Bohm, 8 *tl* Science Photo Library/NASA GSFC/Gene Feldman, *bl* Science Photo Library/CNES,1995 Distribution Spot Image, 8-9 Science Photo Library/Royal Observatory, Edinburgh, *c* Powerstock/Zefa/ Panther, 9 *c* Science Photo Library/US Geological Survey, *cr* Science Photo Library/NASA, *bc* Science Photo Library/Space Telescope Science Institute/Nasa, *br* Science Photo Library/Nasa, 10 *tr* Science Photo Library/NASA, 11 *tr* Planet Earth Pictures/Georgette Douwma, 12 *tl* Mary Evans Picture Library, 13 *tr* Robert Harding Picture Library, 14 *cl* Oxford Scientific Films/Matthias Breiter, *br* Science Photo Library/David Parker, 15 *cl* Robert Harding Picture Library, *br* Science Photo Library/David Parker, 16 *tl* Mary Evans Picture Library, 17 *tr* National Geographic Society/Cartographic Computer Lab/INGS Image Collection, 18 *tl* Jean-Loup Charmet, *bl* Science Photo Library/NASA, 19 *br* Geoscience Features Picture Library, 21 *tr* Science Photo Library/Pekka Parviainen, 22 *tl* Science Photo Library/Simon Fraser, *bl* Science Photo Library/Simon Fraser, 22-23 *b* Tony Stone Images/Wayne Eastep, 23 *tr* Frank Spooner Pictures/Nasa/Liaison/*b* B. Ingalls, 24 *tl* AKG London, *bl* Martin Redfern, 25 *br* Frank Spooner Pictures/Gilles Bassignac, 26 *tl* Werner Forman Archive/British Museum, London, *cl* Robert Harding Picture Library/D. Peebles, 27 *tc* Frank Spooner Pictures/B. Lewis/ *tr* Planet Earth Pictures/Bourseiller & Durieux, *c* Frank Spooner Pictures/A.P.I., *cr* Planet Earth Pictures/Verena Tunnicliffe, 28 *tl* Planet Earth Pictures/Bourseiller - I & V, 28-29 Katz Pictures/Alberto Garcia/SABA, 29 *tr* Frank Lane Picture Agency/USDA Forest Service, *cr* Frank Lane Picture Agency/USDA

Forest Service, *br* Frank Lane Picture Agency/ USDA Forest Service, 30 *tl* Topham Picture Point, *tr* Popperfoto/Reuters/Ted Aljibe, *cl* ET Archive/ Royal Society, *bl* Planet Earth Pictures/Bourseiller - I & V, 31 *tl* Corbis UK/Library of Congress, *tc* Corbis UK/Library of Congress, *tr* Corbis UK/Library of Congress, *cr* Frank Spooner Pictures/Kevin West, *br* Planet Earth Pictures/ Krafft - I & V, 32-33 *c* TRH/US Navy, 33 *cl* Science Photo Library/David Parker, *c* Popperfoto/Reuter, *bc* Popperfoto/Reuters/ Reinhard Krause, 34 *t* Rex Features/Sipa Press, *tl* Peter Newark's Pictures, *clt* John Frost Historical Newspaper Service, *cl* John Frost Historical Newspaper Service, *bl* Popperfoto/Reuter, *br* Popperfoto/Reuter, 34-35 *t* Popperfoto/Reuter, 35 *tr* Tony Stone Images/Warren Bolster, *b* Tony Stone Images/Ed Pritchard, 36 *tl* Science Photo Library/Science Museum, 36-37 *b* Popperfoto, 37 *br* Science Photo Library/David Parker, 38 *tl* Science Photo Library/Martin Bond, *bl* Tony Stone Images/Monica Dalmasso, 40 *tl* Tony Stone Images/Gary Irving, *cr* Corbis UK/Library of Congress, 41 *tl* Frank Spooner Pictures/Shamsi-Basha, *tr* Frank Spooner Pictures/Gamma/ Schofield /Liais, *cl* Oxford Scientific Films/M.P.L. Fogden, *cr* NHPA/Jany Sauvanet, *br* Sygma/Palm Beach Post/Waters, 42 *tc* Oxford Scientific Films/Scott Camazine, *tr* Popperfoto/Reuters/Peter Morgan, *cl* Science Photo Library/NASA, *bl* Science Photo Library/NASA, 43 *tr* Oxford Scientific Films/E.R. Degginger, *cl* The Met Office, *br* Sygma/Bleibtreu /John Hillelson Agency, 44 *tl* Rex Features/Sipa/ Oliver Monn, *bl* Science Photo Library/Pekka Parviainen, 44-45 Popperfoto, 45 *br* Frank Lane Picture Agency/Martin B Withers, 46 Image Bank/Mancle Isy Stewart, *tl* Tony Stone Images, 46-47 *c* Planet Earth Pictures/J.P. Nacivet, *bc* Tony Stone Images/Frans Lanting, 47 *br* NHPA/Anthony Bannister, 48 *tl* Science Photo Library/Dr Jeremy Burgess, *bl* Science Photo Library/NASA, 49 Oxford Scientific Films/Paul Franklin, 50 *tl* Tony Stone Images/Glen Allison, *bl* Tony Stone Images/ Demetrio Carrasco, 51 *c* Tony Stone Images/ Cameron Davidson, 52 *bl* Panos Pictures/Liba Taylor, 53 *c* Science Photo Library/Earth Satellite Corporation, *cr* Science Photo Library/Earth Satellite Corporation, 54 *tl* Mary Evans Picture Library, *bl* Tony Stone Images/Tom Bean, 55 *tr* Tony Stone Images/Arnulf Husmo, *br* Planet Earth Pictures/John Lythgoe, 56 *tl* NHPA/George Bernard, *bl* Planet Earth Pictures/Jon & Alison Moran, 56-57 *c* Science Photo Library/Martin Dohrn, 57 *bc* Frank Spooner Pictures, 58 *tl* Mary Evans Picture Library, *c* The Royal Geographical Society, 59 *tl* Corbis UK/Jim Sugar Photography, *cr* The Natural History

Museum, London, *br* Auscape International Photo Lib. 60 *cr* Corbis UK/James L. Amos, 61 *cl* Simon Conway Morris, University of Cambridge, 62 *tl* Planet Earth Pictures/Steve Hopkin, 62 *tc (background)* Science Photo Library/Kaj R. Svensson, 62 *bl* Planet Earth Pictures/A.S. Edwards, 62-63 *t* Science Photo Library/Manfred Kage, 62-63 *b (background)* Science Photo Library/Kaj R. Svensson, 63 *tc (background)* Science Photo Library/Kaj R. Svensson, 63 *tr* Science Photo Library/Sinclair Stammers, 63 *br* Oxford Scientific Films/Marshall Black, 64 *tr* Planet Earth Pictures/Peter Scoones, 65 *cl* Planet Earth Pictures/Ken Lucas, 66 *cl* The Natural History Museum, London, *cr* Science Photo Library/ Sinclair Stammers, 67 *cl* Science Photo Library/ Sinclair Stammers, 68 *c* Science Photo Library/ Vaughan Fleming, 69 *cr* The Ronald Grant Archive, *bc* The Natural History Museum, London, 70 *tl* Science Photo Library/Geological Survey of Canada/Mark Pilkington, *bl* Science Photo Library/NASA, 71 *cl* Alessandro Montanaii, 73 *cl* Corbis UK/Ecoscene /Sally A. Morgan, *cr* The Natural History Museum, London, 74 *tl* Novosti, 75 *cl* The Natural History Museum, London, *cr* The Natural History Museum, London, 76 *tl* Powerstock/Zefa, *tr* The Natural History Museum, London, 77 *tl* Powerstock/Zefa /Bond, *c* The Natural History Museum, London, *cr* The Natural History Museum, London, *bc* The Natural History Museum, London, *br* The Natural History Museum, London, 78 *cl* Science Photo Library, *bl* Science Photo Library, 79 *cl* Science Photo Library, *br* Science Photo Library, 80 *tl* Science Photo Library/KAJ R. Svensson, 80-81 *t* Science Photo Library/Rosenfeld Images Ltd, 81 *br* Tony Stone Images/Lester Lefkowitz, 82 *tl* Science Photo Library/Vaughan Fleming, *cr* The Natural History Museum, London, *br* The Bridgeman Art Library/ Derby Museum & Art Gallery, 83 *c* NHPA/Anthony Bannister, *cr* Popperfoto/W.U.W, 84 *tl* Martin Redfern, *bl* Tony Stone Images/Philip H. Coblentz, 86 *tl* Tony Stone Images/David Woodfall, 87 *tr* Tony Stone Images/David Woodfall, *cl* Tony Stone Images/Robert Van Der Hils.

Key: b = bottom, c = centre, l = left, r = right, t = top

Every effort has been made to trace the copyright holders of the photographs. The publishers apologize for any inconvenience caused.

The publishers would also like to thank the following: Clarissa Claudel, Peter Clayman, Pauline Newman, Robin Redfern, Marc Wilson.

QVADRATVS PRI

TRIGONVS TPILONOS SEV MV

TRIGONVS

VM TRI

PISCIBVS

ORBIS TE

SAII

ET

ORBIS

TIO PLA N ETARVM

EODEM SIGNO.

E

SCORPIO DISTANTI

MAR

TRILO

CRO ASPICI

TRIGON ASPICE IN

LIBRAE SE IN TEGRIS